Library of
Davidson College

POLICY PAPERS
IN INTERNATIONAL AFFAIRS
*
NUMBER EIGHT

U.S. FOREIGN POLICY IN SUB-SAHARAN AFRICA: NATIONAL INTEREST AND GLOBAL STRATEGY

ROBERT M. PRICE

INSTITUTE OF INTERNATIONAL STUDIES
UNIVERSITY OF CALIFORNIA
BERKELEY

In sponsoring the Policy Papers in International Affairs series, the Institute of International Studies reasserts its commitment to a vigorous policy debate by providing a forum for innovative approaches to important policy issues. The views expressed in each paper are those of the author only, and publication in this series does not constitute endorsement by the Institute.

International Standard Book Number 0-87725-508-3

Library of Congress Card Number 78-65499

© 1978 by the Regents of the University of California

CONTENTS

I. AFRICA POLICY: KISSINGER AND CARTER	1
II. U.S. TANGIBLE INTERESTS IN SUB-SAHARAN AFRICA	6
1. U.S. Security Interests	6
2. U.S. Economic Interests	14
Policy Implications of Economic Interests	20
III. GLOBAL CONSIDERATIONS IN AFRICA POLICY	30
Credibility and Power	32
U.S. Credibility and Soviet/Cuban Involvement in Africa	35
Angola and Ethiopia	36
Rhodesia/Zimbabwe	41
Zaire	51
IV. CONCLUSION	59
NOTES	67

I

AFRICA POLICY: KISSINGER AND CARTER

In the early days of the Carter administration public attention was drawn to a supposedly new orientation in the making of U.S. foreign policy. Cold War stereotypes were to be discarded. No longer would policy be simply reactive, premised primarily on the behavior —actual or predicted—of the Communist powers. Public attention was drawn to this "new orientation" particularly with regard to sub-Saharan Africa when, in marked contrast to the foreign policy spokesmen of the previous administration, UN Ambassador Andrew Young stated that he considered the Cuban presence in Angola a positive factor—a force for stability there. Thus it is especially ironic that by the midpoint of its first term, the Carter administration's Africa policy should be dominated by the "danger" of Cuban/Soviet involvement in the African continent. As that involvement expanded from Angola to the Horn of Africa, as the number of Cuban troops south of the Sahara increased to an estimated forty thousand, and as the Cuban military assumed a significant combat role in the Ogaden region of Ethiopia, a major concern within the Carter administration became how best to respond to this Communist "intervention" so as to check the spread of Soviet/Cuban influence in sub-Saharan Africa. This concern has been heightened by the possibility of an expanded Soviet and Cuban role not only in Ethiopia, but also in southern Africa and Zaire. In all three areas there is uncertainty about what the Cubans and Soviets are likely to do, but developments point to expanded involvement as a decided possibility. In Ethiopia, the deployment of Cuban advisors and combat troops suggests preparation for them to play a significant role in the Eritrean fighting.* In southern Africa, the efforts by the

---

*There are, at the same time, significant indications that the Cubans have resisted pressure from the Ethiopian government to involve them in the military campaign against the Eritrean secessionists. There are good reasons for them to resist—e.g., their previous support of one of the two main Eritrean movements, the fact that many of their friends and allies continue to consider the Eritrean struggle a just cause, and the difficulties of waging conventional warfare in the mountainous Eritrean terrain.

Smith regime to institutionalize an "internal settlement" in Rhodesia, the apparent inability of the Patriotic Front to press its military advantage to a clear and rapid battlefield victory, and the consequent economic and political vulnerability of the Kaunda regime in Zambia —all raise the possibility that the Soviets and particularly the Cubans will become directly involved so as to decisively tip the military balance toward the Zimbabwe liberation groups.* Finally in Zaire, the vulnerability of the U.S.-supported Mobutu regime, manifested by its utter incapacity to cope with insurgents returning to their homeland from neighboring Angola, led the Carter administration to charge the Cubans with involvement in that country and to raise the spectre of Soviet designs on one of the most mineral-rich pieces of real estate on the African continent.

The earliest (and still clearest) official description of the Soviet/Cuban "threat" in sub-Saharan Africa was made by Secretary of State Kissinger in a statement before the Senate Subcommittee on African Affairs. Testifying in March 1976, he offered the following analysis and prognosis:

> Late last year the situation in Africa took on a new and serious dimension. . . . The Soviets and Cubans had imposed their solution on Angola. Their forces were entrenched there, and fresh opportunities lay before them. . . . With the end of the Portuguese era in Africa, pressure was building on Rhodesia. . . . Events in Angola encouraged radicals to press for a military solution in Rhodesia. . . . With radical influence on the rise, and with immense outside military strength apparently behind the radicals, even moderate and responsible African leaders . . . began to conclude there was no alternative but to embrace the cause of violence. By March of this year [1976] guerrilla actions had begun to break out against Rhodesia. . . . The possibility grew of an emerging pattern of accommodation to the reality of Soviet presence and American inaction. We saw ahead the prospect of war—which indeed had already begun—fed by outside forces; we were concerned about a continent politically embittered and economically estranged from the West; and we saw ahead a process of radicalization which would place severe strains on our allies in Europe and Japan.[1]

*A recent State Department announcement on U.S. policy in Rhodesia states: "Soviet and Cuban intervention is a strong possibility if the conflict continues, and U.S. interests would suffer" (U.S. Department of State, Bureau of Public Affairs, "Rhodesia: U.S. Policy," *Gist*, June 1978).

Although the Secretary did not explicitly set out the implications of this trend of events for the Republic of South Africa, the logic of his argument is clear. If radicals backed by the Soviet Union successfully used violence to come to power in Rhodesia, insurgent violence could be expected in South Africa. Just as radical triumphs in Angola and Mozambique had precipitated the new situation in Rhodesia, once the radicals were entrenched in Zimbabwe, "fresh opportunities" would "lay before them."

The policy that Kissinger fashioned to meet the perceived threat of spreading Soviet influence under the auspices of African radicalism was to orchestrate, through diplomacy and political pressure, a "moderate" political solution in Rhodesia. The Angolan experience had taught the Secretary of State that Congress could not be counted on to support a direct U.S. response to the Soviet Union in Africa; the "moderate solution" emerged as a means to halt the development of those trends that would call for such a response. If insurgency was the avenue for the spread of Soviet power, then the U.S. would use its influence to simultaneously end the guerrilla war and replace the white minority regime that had spawned it with a government based upon a "peaceful" transition to majority rule. Thus a radical transformation of Zimbabwe would be prevented and the concomitant Soviet threat blocked.

The newly elected Carter administration, with perhaps some reservations, adopted the essentials of the Kissinger policy, now modified into the Anglo-American Plan for Zimbabwe. Thus in Spring 1977 Ambassador Young, testifying before the Senate upon his return from southern Africa, stated that "there really is no clear break [with the Kissinger policy] and completely new initiative.... It is much more an evolution from that policy." He went on to testify about U.S. goals with respect to Rhodesia:

> I think I would say that our policy is not just majority rule, but a commitment to move as rapidly as possible to achieve a transfer to majority rule without violence, or with a minimum of violence .... in order to keep the resources that we require from Africa coming to us uninterrupted, it requires a certain level of peace and reasonableness in the change process.[2]

In contrast to the public statements of Secretary of State Kissinger, the emphasis here is on avoiding "violence" rather than on a specifically Soviet or Communist threat. This should be seen as a difference in form—not substance, however. For the underlying assumptions and resultant logic of the Young statement are similar to those which buttressed and shaped policy under previous administrations—namely, that "violence" (a code word for insurgent movements) is the midwife of radically dominated or influenced governments and that such governments would be a threat to the ability of the U.S. to obtain "the resources that we require from Africa."*

The statement of Ambassador Young before the Senate Subcommittee on African Affairs stands in obvious contradiction to his stated belief that the Cuban presence in Angola was not a threat to the U.S., but rather a force for stability. Contradictions such as this, reflected in the statement of a single official, appear to be a fundamental aspect of foreign policy-making under the Carter administration. Two tendencies vie with each other: on the one hand, there is the sense that the policy paradigm which governed the conduct of U.S. foreign affairs since World War II, and the interventionist posture that flowed from it, are no longer appropriate to contemporary global realities; on the other hand, there is the view that the Soviet Union continues to be the *major* threat to the U.S. and that the assumptions and action orientations that governed U.S. efforts to "contain" that threat are still, in their essentials, valid. These two opposing perspectives, supported by different factions within the policy elite, and in some cases unreconciled in the thought of the same individual, may in part be responsible for the incoherence perceived by many observers in the foreign policy of the Carter administration.

However significant the first, or "non-interventionist," perspective was at the beginning of the Carter administration, there is good reason to believe that the second, or what may be thought of as the "neo-containment" orientation, was from the outset likely to emerge as the dominant tendency. It is, after all, supported by the assumptions of twentieth-century American political culture, and has well-entrenched constituencies in the Executive bureaucracy, the Congress, the defense and intelligence communities, and the public. Not surprisingly then, the increasing involvement of the Soviet Union and Cuba in the affairs of sub-Saharan Africa has precipitated a rapid shift in orientation toward a perspective in which the actions

*It is of course possible that the intense concern of the Carter administration to avoid a violent solution in Rhodesia grows out of an abhorrence of violence by its members and a belief that historically nothing worthwhile has developed from it. This would be a rather peculiar perspective to be adopted by the government of a country which itself was born in armed conflict, and which celebrates that violent struggle each year. Even stranger would be the involvement of the U.S. government in a far-off continent in order to put into practice the pacifist beliefs of administration personnel.

of the Communist powers are the central consideration in U.S. policy toward that region. Thus the assessment that current Soviet/Cuban behavior in Africa is sufficiently threatening to the U.S. that it should be countered now appears to be nearly universally accepted among U.S. policymakers, and has become a persistent theme in the public statements of the President, his National Security Advisor, and the Secretary of State.

The purpose of this paper is to subject this assessment to careful scrutiny. I will be concerned primarily with two sorts of questions. First: What is the nature of U.S. interests in sub-Saharan Africa, and in what ways are these interests threatened by current Cuban/Soviet activity? Second: What effective options are available to the U.S. to counter increased Cuban and Soviet involvement?

The current Cuban/Soviet involvement in sub-Saharan Africa, and its possible expansion southward, is generally thought to pose two types of threat to the U.S. The first is a threat to certain tangible interests of a military/strategic and economic kind. The second is a threat to the U.S. global position—an undermining of U.S. credibility as a great, or world, power. Each of these types of "threat" will be dealt with in turn.

II

U.S. TANGIBLE INTERESTS IN SUB-SAHARAN AFRICA

U.S. SECURITY INTERESTS

Concern with U.S. interests of a security or strategic nature in sub-Saharan Africa is focused almost entirely on the vulnerability of Western shipping lanes in the Indian Ocean and around the Cape of Good Hope. It is often pointed out that almost all of Western Europe's oil supply and a major portion of U.S. oil imports are carried in these shipping lanes, and that by blockading them the Soviet Union could rapidly apply an economic stranglehold on the Western alliance. Thus possible access by the Soviet Navy to basing facilities on the Horn of Africa, in South Africa, and (to a lesser extent) on the East African coast is viewed with great alarm by some, who see them as providing the means for such a blockade. The existence of a now defunct Soviet naval base at Berbera in Somalia and the possibility that Soviet/Cuban involvement in Ethiopia could provide the Soviets with a base at the Eritrean port of Massawa have drawn attention to the Horn of Africa because it is feared that such bases could be used to blockade oil tankers from moving from the Persian Gulf through the Red Sea to the Suez Canal. At the same time, the political turmoil in southern Africa, with the concomitant "radicalization" of the politics of the area, and the potential for Cuban/Soviet direct support for the Zimbabwe insurgents have drawn increased attention to the Cape Oil Route. Because the supertankers carrying the bulk of Western petroleum imports from the Persian Gulf are too large to navigate the Suez Canal, and because the Canal can in any case easily be closed, most of the oil bound for Europe and the U.S. travels south through the Indian Ocean passing around the Cape of Good Hope into the Atlantic. Consequently, the security of these shipping lanes is of vital importance to the West. In strategic thinking regarding this "Cape Route," much has been made of the role of the Republic of South Africa (particularly the modern Smithstown naval facility there). As one authority on these matters puts it:

For nearly two hundred years the critical strategic importance of the Cape to the Western trading system has been generally recognized. . . . In the age of the Cape Oil Route, the strategic significance of the best intermediary position between Europe and India is even further enhanced. . . . Consolidation of Soviet influence in South Africa would almost certainly be the penultimate stage in the economic strangulation of the West. . . . South Africa's strategic integrity is thus clearly vital for the defence and even the survival of the West.[3]

The implication drawn by proponents of this view is that it is strategically necessary to avoid a political transformation in South Africa that might produce an African radical regime—especially one that comes to power with Soviet assistance.

The strategic concerns expressed in what might be termed the "Cape Route Doctrine" are directly relevant to South Africa alone, and would appear therefore to be somewhat remote from immediate policy considerations. However, those who share this perspective see the unfolding Rhodesia/Zimbabwe drama as vitally, if indirectly, related, and foresee an important strategic threat should the Patriotic Front come to power with direct Cuban/Soviet involvement. The logic underlying this perception can be found in the views of former Secretary of State Kissinger as expressed to the Senate Subcommittee on African Affairs (see p. 2 above). A radical transformation of neighboring Rhodesia is seen as providing an important destabilizing effect on South Africa, creating the context and pretext for increased Soviet influence in (and perhaps eventual domination of) South Africa: "Victory for the Russians on the ruins of white rule in Rhodesia . . . would have incalculable results for Western interests and influence in Southern Africa as a whole."[4] Thus within the strategic perspective associated with the Cape Route Doctrine, the maintenance of U.S. interests in the Republic of South Africa is dependent upon the maintenance of a pro-Western, "moderate" government in Rhodesia/Zimbabwe.

This strategic paradigm, within which a significant threat to U.S. security interests is currently seen to exist in Africa—particularly in southern Africa and the Horn—is based upon an interlocking set of political and military/technical suppositions. These are usually asserted as self-evident truths, but can be shown to be seriously flawed both logically and empirically.

To begin with, there is the notion that a radical regime coming to power in Africa with aid from the Soviet Union will as a matter of course be so subject to Soviet influence that it will allow its ports

to be used as bases for offensive naval operations against the West. To be sustained, this view must severely discount the significance of nationalism in the outlook of radical African governments. However, recent historical experience has shown that African radical regimes in particular, for a variety of reasons involving considerations of domestic and foreign politics, tend to be especially concerned with projecting an image of self-reliance and sovereignty. Once firmly in charge, such regimes are not likely to be sanguine about dramatic demonstrations of their subservience to an outside power. And perhaps nothing symbolizes such subservience more forcefully than the establishment by a foreign state of a large and permanent military installation. The post-independence record of Angola and Mozambique should undermine any assumption that Soviet/Cuban-backed radical regimes will automatically become the hosts to substantial Soviet military bases. Despite considerable comment in the West about the potential threat posed by the port facilities existing in these two countries, the fact is that there is no evidence of significant movement toward the establishment of Soviet naval facilities in these newly independent, Marxist-oriented states. In the case of Mozambique, the Soviets apparently made overtures concerning naval facilities shortly after independence, but these were pointedly and publicly rebuffed by the new government.[5]*
In Angola the Soviet position should be stronger than it is in Mozambique, given the decisive importance of Soviet military assistance in the MPLA victory there. Nevertheless, the Angolan leaders have indicated their unwillingness to adopt a client or satellite status vis-à-vis the Soviets. Thus on the occasion of the signing of a Treaty of Friendship between Angola and the USSR, the Angolan President Antonio Agostinho Neto took the opportunity to proclaim that "Angola belongs to the group of nonaligned countries, so it has no intention of joining any military bloc. . . ."[6] In a similar vein, an advisor to Mozambique President Samora Machel told a prominent American journalist that "we don't intend to become another Bulgaria here and we certainly don't want to get involved in bloc politics."[7]

*There have been reports emanating from South Africa that the Soviets were constructing a military base on Mozambique's Bazaruto island, but these have been vehemently denied by Mozambique authorities. In response to the charges the government flew Western diplomats, including the U.S. ambassador, over the island to prove the reports false. However, consent has apparently been granted for Soviet warships to visit Mozambique and Angolan ports (see David Ottaway, " 'Afrocommunism' Seen as New Force in Mozambique," *Washington Post*, February 16, 1977).

U.S. SECURITY INTERESTS

In addition to discounting the role of nationalism, the "Cape Route" strategic paradigm fails to take into account the *character* of the ties that exist between liberation movements or "radical" governments and the Communist states. In Africa, these ties are predicated far more on instrumental than on ideological considerations. Thus the external ties of the liberation movements in southern Africa are primarily the result of the willingness of the East to offer material and psychological support while the West was attending to its tangible interests in Africa and to the cohesion of the NATO alliance.* Political and military ties built on instrumental considerations are highly labile, as has been dramatically illustrated by the rapid dismantling of the Soviet presence in Ghana [1966], Sudan [1971], Egypt [1975], and now Somalia [1978]. What these examples point to is the extreme fragility of Soviet influence in African and third world states. Given the limited commitment to Marxism in most such states, their susceptibility to nationalism, and their considerable developmental difficulties, an overriding lesson of recent history would seem to be that the Soviet Union is unable to sustain its influence when it is challenged by the West on instrumental grounds—i.e., in the provision of capital, technological assistance, access to export markets, and the like.

In sum, then, the political assumptions underlying the automatic equation of radical regimes with a Soviet security threat are seriously flawed. Let us, however, for the moment ignore this and accept a worst-case analysis—that Soviet/Cuban activity will help to produce a consolidated military regime in Addis Ababa and a radical African government in Pretoria which will permit the establishment of extensive Soviet naval installations on their territories. Even granting this, it is far from clear that a genuine threat to Western shipping lanes would exist. For in order to sustain the argument that Africa's ports are of strategic significance to the West, it is necessary to make a number of not very plausible assumptions about Soviet intentions and capabilities. Is it realistic to assume that even if the Soviet Union had complete access to naval facilities on the Horn and in South Africa, it would and could in fact use them as bases for blockading Western oil shipments?

*In the conventional view, political instability is the primary threat to tangible interests, and thus their protection dictates support for the political status quo. Since Angola and Mozambique were Portuguese colonies and Portugal was a member of NATO, considerations of alliance politics inhibited the U.S. from supporting the anti-Portuguese independence movements and from denying Portugal the military materiel it needed to pursue its counterinsurgency efforts in Africa.

In a recent analysis, Tom Farer has persuasively demonstrated that the idea of a threat to Western shipping lanes from ports on the Horn is highly implausible.[8] He reasons that such an action would be neither cost-effective relative to alternatively available means, nor rational with regard to overall global considerations. The arguments made by Farer concerning the Horn can be applied with equal weight to southern Africa, where a number of additional factors make the notion of a Soviet naval threat even less plausible.

Any attempt to argue that Soviet access to African ports would pose a threat to oil shipments to the West involves a presupposition regarding Soviet intentions. Is it conceivable, given the global realities of the fourth quarter of the twentieth century, that the Soviets would seriously contemplate blockading vital Western oil shipments? Such a direct act of war against the Western industrialized world would most likely precipitate World War III, making the flow of petroleum an utterly irrelevant issue. Either the ensuing military conflict would be rapidly settled through negotiation, in which case there would be no need for oil in transit since Western stocks would suffice, or the conflict would be "nuclearized," in which case there would also be no need for the blockaded oil shipments, their destinations having ceased to exist. In either case, the events precipitated by the initiation of a blockade would immediately render oil irrelevant. Thus if the Soviets wished to begin World War III, it is hardly plausible that they would do so by interdicting Western shipping from bases in sub-Saharan Africa. But let us once again ignore the implausibility of the assumptions underlying the case for the strategic importance of Africa's ports, and accept that an oil blockade is something the Soviet Union would reasonably contemplate. What of the technical aspects involved in implementing such an action?

If the Soviets wished to stop the flow of petroleum from the Persian Gulf, there are far more efficient means for them to do so than to mount a naval blockade from ports in the Horn (Ethiopia, Somalia, Djibouti) and/or southern Africa.* To begin with, the objective of stopping the Persian Gulf oil flow could be most ef-

---

*The strategic significance attributed to the ports on Africa's Horn is based upon their location near the entrance to the Red Sea, from which it is possible to control access to the southern entrance to the Suez Canal. As far as Western shipping is concerned, this is of only very marginal significance, however, since the Cape Route is a viable alternative to Suez. The Cape Route was used during the lengthy period of the Canal's closure following the Six-Day War, and is currently utilized by the supertankers carrying the bulk of the West's oil. This, of course, is why the southern African port facilities are deemed so strategically important.

ficiently accomplished by non-naval means. Bombing the oil fields, arranging for their sabotage, or military occupation of the key oil-producing countries all seem preferable on a "cost-benefit" basis. Each of these could be accomplished more swiftly and easily and with a more complete effect than the continuing maintenance of a naval blockade.[9] Furthermore, such methods have the decided advantage of being indirect, rather than direct, acts of war against the Western powers. But even if the Soviets decided to use naval power to interdict oil shipments, they would be unlikely to mount such an operation from bases in sub-Saharan Africa. A blockade of the shipping lanes around the Cape from South African bases is particularly unlikely because it would require effective patrolling of thousands of miles of high seas between the Cape of Good Hope and Antarctica. A more rational target area for a blockade would be the Strait of Hormuz, at the mouth of the Persian Gulf.[10] Thus South African bases make little sense with respect to an Indian Ocean interdiction. Bases on the Horn, being much closer to the Persian Gulf, might appear a more serious threat. However, as Tom Farer has pointed out, "interdiction in the Mediterranean and the North Atlantic" offers "numerous advantages over an Indian Ocean exercise. . . ." Occurring in an area proximate to European Russia, an Atlantic-Mediterranean operation would offer the Soviets shorter lines of supply, the opportunity for vastly superior air cover, easier access to major repair facilities, and the like.[11] It would also permit a rapid shift in mission objectives from interdiction to strategic defense—an extremely important advantage to which we shall return later.

The use of African bases by the Soviets would not only be more costly and less effective than available alternatives, but such bases would also be particularly vulnerable to Western attack. Soviet naval facilities on the Horn, on the East African coast, and in South Africa which were being used to support an Indian Ocean-Cape Route blockade could easily be destroyed by U.S. carrier-based air power, and the same task force could be used to provide the necessary protection for shipping. The U.S. capacity to launch and sustain such operations would not be undermined by the denial of African bases to the West. The fact that the United States has a "blue water navy" —i.e., a naval capacity that is essentially free of land-based logistical anchors—means that it can project its own power and check the power of other states without the necessity of access to ports such as those in sub-Saharan Africa. And in the unlikely event that sea-based facilities were not sufficient to handle the Soviet presence (which would itself face very severe resupply problems), the U.S. has a substantial base available at Diego Garcia in the Indian Ocean.*

The technical deficiencies of an Indian Ocean-based interdiction of Persian Gulf oil are not the only considerations rendering such an action highly irrational from the Soviet vantage point. Important strategic considerations add to the difficulties of such an operation. Most qualified observers of Soviet naval expansion agree that the Soviet navy has developed in response to the nuclear threat posed by the U.S. carrier task forces and submarine-launched ballistic missiles, and that thus its primary task is to provide strategic defense of the Soviet heartland.[12]† To deploy their submarine fleet so as to interdict Western shipping between the Persian Gulf and the waters off the Cape, they would have to accept a fundamental weakening in their navy's capacity to carry out this primary strategic responsibility. This becomes especially clear when the notion of a Soviet move to interdict Western oil supplies is put in realistic international perspective. Since such a move would be considered a major act of war directed against all the Western industrial states, Soviet strategists would have to confront the likelihood that it would be a prelude to a major conventional (and quite possibly nuclear) war. Under such circumstances, at least two considerations would become paramount to them: (1) Europe would be a major, if not the primary, theater of any conventional war fought between the USSR and the West, and (2) since there could be no guarantee that the enemy would remain within the bounds of conventional warfare, the Soviet defense against nuclear attack must be on alert. The first consideration—the possibility of a ground war in Europe—would necessitate the deployment of Soviet naval power in the North

---

*Carrier task forces can be resupplied and refueled at the Diego Garcia base, its airfields can accommodate the full range of planes in the U.S. arsenal, and it is the only U.S. facility in the region at which the P-3C Orion anti-submarine warfare plane and the KC-135 tanker plane are based. (The former is important for control of the ocean depths, and the latter can refuel B-52 bombers in flight.) In addition, Diego Garcia offers a potential port for submarines.

†From the Soviet point of view, the establishment of naval bases on the Horn of Africa has a strategic function in response to the deployment of Polaris A-3, Poseidon, and Trident submarine-launched ballistic missiles (SLBMs) by the U.S. These SLBMs are capable of reaching targets in the Soviet heartland from the northwest quadrant of the Indian Ocean (the Arabian Sea), and the Soviet naval bases on the Horn, which is adjacent to the Arabian Sea, could be used to protect against such attacks. Thus the motivation of the Soviets in establishing a base like Berbera can be explained more plausibly as defensive than as creating the capability for an attack on Western shipping (see Farer, p. 105).

Atlantic and Mediterranean to prevent supplies originating in the United States from reaching U.S. and allied troops. (This, of course, reinforces the point that if the Soviets wished to blockade Western oil shipments, they could do so best in the North Atlantic and Mediterranean, which is not only a logistically superior area, but would also allow for the strategic placement of the Soviet fleet to meet the global contingencies stemming from the interdiction itself. That is something that a blockade in the Indian Ocean would not allow.)

The second consideration—the expansion of a conventional war into a nuclear conflict—enters in because however much Soviet strategists may believe that a conflict sparked by their action to interdict oil supply lines can be prevented from "going nuclear," it would be insanity for them to ignore the possibility. Thus they would be concerned with deploying their navy for the defense of the Soviet heartland against nuclear weapons. Since the overall thrust of their recent naval expansion is directed precisely toward countering a submarine and carrier-borne nuclear attack, it is reasonable to assume that in a situation of extreme danger—such as would be created by a Soviet oil blockade—their naval forces would be appropriately deployed to meet such an attack.[13] That is, they would be deployed in the areas from which a U.S. sea-launched nuclear attack would be initiated—the Mediterranean, the North Atlantic and North Sea, and perhaps the Arabian Sea—and not thousands of miles away in the Indian Ocean and off the Cape of Good Hope in search of oil tankers. Therefore, even if we assume the unlikely possibility that the Soviet Union would be willing to run the grave risk of major conventional war (or even nuclear conflict) in order to interdict Western oil shipments, we discover that the interdiction of the Cape Oil Route from bases on the African continent would, from the Soviet vantage point, be strategically untenable. The conditions of global war which would almost certainly result from the act of interdiction would turn the implementation of a Cape Route blockade into an act of strategic suicide.

On careful examination, then, the "security of shipping lanes doctrine" turns out to be based on an interlocking set of dubious assumptions concerning the relationship between radicalization and Soviet influence in Africa, on the one hand, and the nature of Soviet capabilities and motives, on the other. Thus, the argument that pro-Western governments in southern Africa and on the Horn are vital to the security of the West because of the proximity of these areas to the oil shipping lanes cannot be sustained.

U.S. FOREIGN POLICY IN SUB-SAHARAN AFRICA

This does not mean, however, that Soviet access to the ports in these regions would be of no significance whatsoever. Such a development can be correctly viewed as enhancing, to a degree, the image and reality of the Soviet Union as a great, or global, power. It would symbolize the Soviet presence, and might facilitate the protection of Soviet clients in the area from amphibious attack or naval blockade by Western powers. These would seem to be Soviet advantages which would be of little demonstrable consequence to the *security* of the U.S. Moreover, the significance of such bases for the protection of Soviet allies in Africa is open to question. Note that without bases in Africa the Soviets were apparently able to provide naval cover for supply ships ferrying arms to Angola in 1976, and more recently they have been able to deliver massive supplies of equipment to Ethiopia.

U.S. ECONOMIC INTERESTS

In contrast to the military dimension, where alleged U.S. national interests turned out to be largely illusory, there can be little doubt that the United States and its allies have very tangible economic interests in sub-Saharan Africa. Before turning to an analysis of these interests, one caveat should be noted. In any analysis of the foreign policy implications of economic ties, it is exceedingly important to keep in mind the distinction between private and public (i.e., national) interests. The criteria separating the two do not reside in the question of legal ownership, but rather in a determination of whether a threat to the interest in question would have a significant impact on the continued functioning of a nation's economic system. Thus the nationalization of a corporation or group of corporations involves a threat to private interests only, unless the companies nationalized comprise such a proportion of a state's productive capacity that the action will have an important impact on GNP, employment, and the like. Of course it is quite proper for a government to facilitate the operations of its businessmen abroad, but such aid should stop short of the sacrifice of significant diplomatic-political, military, or other such interests. In this sense we can say that the existence of important private economic interests abroad should not be the basis of a state's foreign policy.

Statistics on U.S. trade and foreign investments indicate that sub-Saharan Africa has a very limited economic significance for the United States. Only 3 percent of U.S. direct investments abroad are found there, and the region purchases a similarly small proportion of total U.S. exports. However, if we break down the aggregate data, certain African countries do appear to possess significance both in terms of the quantity of transactions occurring between them and the U.S. and the particular character of what the U.S. purchases from them. The most significant states in this regard are South Africa, Nigeria, and Zaire. It is in the Republic of South Africa that U.S. economic ties are the most extensive—that country being the recipient of roughly 30 percent of U.S. exports to and 40 percent of U.S. direct investments in sub-Saharan Africa.* Therefore, this analysis of U.S. economic interests in Africa will begin with the South African connection.

Let us look first at the area of investments. Approximately four hundred U.S. firms have invested some $1.5 billion in South African companies, most of which are wholly-owned subsidiaries. To this can be added outstanding loans by U.S. banks to private companies and the South African government totaling $2.2 billion in 1976.[14] The corporations involved in direct investment activity are among the largest U.S. firms: nine of the ten largest firms on *Fortune*'s list of "Top Five Hundred" U.S. corporations have investments in South Africa; overall, 136 of the U.S. firms investing there are on the *Fortune* list.[15] Although these economic links are impressive both in terms of the dollar figures involved and the nature of the U.S. economic institutions represented, they must be seen as constituting private and not public interests because the magnitude of the capital involved is marginal in relation to the total U.S. overseas investments. Only 1.12 percent of U.S. overseas private direct investment is located in South Africa, and South Africa receives only 1.25 percent of the total foreign loans written by U.S. banks. Thus even in the unlikely event of expropriation of all U.S. capital invested in South Africa, the U.S. economy would not be profoundly affected. It might be argued that while the overall economy would not be greatly harmed, some of the most important U.S. corporations would be damaged, with negative effects on the nation in the areas of employment, the maintenance of R & D efforts, and the like. However, further examination reveals that, on the whole, these firms have

---

*Due to U.S. purchases of petroleum, Nigeria is the top exporter to the United States in sub-Saharan Africa, but its imports from the U.S. and the amount of direct investment by U.S. firms are considerably below South African levels. South Africa imports twice as much from the U.S. as Nigeria, and receives three times as much U.S. investment. For statistics on U.S. trade and investment, see U.S. Department of Commerce, *Survey of Current Business* (annual), and *UN Commodity Statistics*, Statistical Papers, Series D.

only marginal proportions of their operations in South Africa. Thus a loss of the capital invested in South Africa would not even dramatically affect *private* U.S. economic interests. Table 1 gives an indication of the minimal role that South African operations play in the overall activities of some of America's major corporations.

Turning from investments to the export side of trade relations, we find a similar picture. In 1976 the United States sold $1.3 billion worth of goods to South Africa, which represented only about 1.5

Table 1

PERCENTAGE OF OPERATIONS OF SELECTED U.S. CORPORATIONS IN SOUTH AFRICA: 1976

Corporation	Percent of Total Assets	Percent of Total Profits	Percent of Total Sales
IBM	‹0.5 %	—	‹1.0%
Caterpillar	‹1.0	—	2.4
General Electric	‹0.5	—	‹0.5
Dow	.0004	‹1.0%	‹1.0
Eastman Kodak	—	‹1.0	‹1.0
3M	—	‹1.0	‹1.0
Warner-Lambert	‹1.0	‹1.0	‹1.0
Pfizer	‹0.5	—	‹0.5
Squibb	‹1.0	1.0	1.0
General Motors	—	—	‹1.0
Ford Motor Company	—	0.3	0.8
Xerox	—	—	0.5
Goodyear	›1.0	—	1.0
Del Monte	1.0	‹1.0	‹1.0
Control Data	0.7	[Loss]	0.7
ITT	—	—	‹1.0
Union Carbide	—	—	0.5

Source: Report to the Board of Regents, University of California (Committee on Investments), September 15, 1977, pp. 47-48. Data are based on responses of corporations to questionnaire sent by Treasurer of Board of Regents.

percent of total U.S. exports. Once again, then, the loss of the South African market to particular American firms might be costly to them, but would have little discernible effect on the overall U.S. economy. Thus, with respect to U.S. export interests, South Africa must be seen as the location of private rather than public, or national, interests.

It is on the import side of trade relations with South Africa that public economic interests emerge for the United States. The U.S. and its allies—Western Europe and Japan—are dependent on imports for a variety of mineral resources that are essential to the production process of highly industrialized economies. In respect to these critical materials, South Africa possesses a major share of the world's known reserves, and produces a significant proportion of the world's supply. As a consequence, the United States and its allies must not only import these minerals, but must do so, to an extensive degree, from the Republic of South Africa.

The U.S. produces no chromite, no manganese, and insufficient quantities of industrial diamonds, nickel, platinum, vanadium, antimony, vermiculite, and certain types of asbestos for its industrial needs. Chromite, vanadium, and antimony are crucial to the production of alloyed steels such as stainless steel, which because of their anti-corrosive properties are essential in high technology industry— especially in the chemical and nuclear energy sectors. At present South Africa produces approximately one-quarter of the world's chrome and antimony and about half of its vanadium.[16] Its reserves of chromite represent almost 80 percent of the world's known resources of that mineral. The United States currently must import approximately 90 percent of its chromite,* 40 percent of its vanadium, and 50 percent of its antimony;[17] and of these imports, 27 percent, 57 percent, and 41 percent respectively come from South Africa.[18] The absence of readily available substitutes for these materials and the peculiar distribution of the world reserves and production suggest that the importance of South Africa as a source for meeting U.S. needs cannot feasibly be eliminated and, indeed, is likely to increase. Ironically, outside of South Africa the only major deposits of chromite and vanadium are found in the Soviet Union, and the only substantial reserves of antimony are in the People's Republic of China. Thus for the U.S. to be cut off from South African imports would involve a serious strategic risk. This risk would be twofold. The first is the obvious one that a traditional

---

*The remainder is produced through reprocessing.

rival would be in a position to withhold vital resources to achieve political ends. The second risk is less obvious, but perhaps more significant. It relates to the structure of the Soviet and Chinese economies. Since these are not export-oriented economies, government investment policies cannot be counted on to expand production of the minerals in question so as to keep pace with world demand. Consequently, there is a real danger of insufficient productive capacity to meet external demand should the industrial world become solely reliant on the Soviet Union and China for its supplies of chromite, vanadium, and antimony. This would not be the result of malevolent political design, but rather of the internal logic of the political economies of the two countries. It would seem, then, that U.S. national interest dictates continued importation of materials necessary to the production of specialty steels from sources other than the planned economies, and that means from South Africa.

Although access to minerals essential to alloyed steel production represents the most important U.S. public economic interest in South Africa, access to a number of other natural resources found there is still significant, if less critical. This is true of the platinum group metals, which are essential in current technology for pollution control and thus in increasing demand in the industrial world; of crocidolite asbestos, which is important in the manufacture of cement; of industrial diamonds; and of manganese. South Africa possesses two-thirds of the world's platinum reserves, it is responsible for over three-quarters of the non-Communist world's production, and it supplies roughly one-quarter of current U.S. needs.[19] Crocidolite asbestos is produced only in South Africa, and thus the U.S. must import its supply entirely from there.[20] Industrial grade diamonds, which one authoritative source describes as "so important that a deficiency . . . would cause a breakdown in the modern metalworking industry and devastate mass production,"[21] are not produced within the United States; approximately half of the U.S. supply comes from South Africa,* which contributes a sizable proportion of the world's output.[22]

---

*U.S. Department of State, *The Trade Debate*, 1978. Figures for U.S. imports of industrial diamonds vary widely. One reason for this is that a significant proportion of these diamonds is imported *indirectly* from South Africa. Thus the Department of the Interior's *Mining & Minerals Policy*, 1977, reports industrial diamonds imported from Ireland, Belgium-Lux, and the U.K., but notes that the diamonds from these three countries are "probably of Republic of South Africa origin." On this basis, the Interior Department's statistics indicate that fully 81 percent of U.S. industrial diamond imports originate in South Africa.

U.S. ECONOMIC INTERESTS

The U.S. dependency on South Africa for minerals is replicated in exaggerate form by its closest allies among the industrial states—Britain, France, Germany, and Japan. In addition to the minerals which the U.S. must import, these countries depend on South African supplies to cover needs which the United States covers wholly or in large part from domestic mineral production. Thus South Africa supplies over 40 percent of Japan's uranium requirements, and is becoming increasingly important as a source of this strategic material for France and Germany. Given the importance of nuclear energy as a substitute for fossil-based fuels, and with South Africa accounting for 20 percent of the world's known uranium reserves, we can expect reliance on South African supplies to increase.[23]

As was noted earlier, the reliance of the U.S. on sub-Saharan Africa for its supply of critical industrial resources goes beyond the Republic of South Africa. The U.S. relies on imports for 97 percent of its cobalt, of which Zaire supplies approximately half.[24] Zaire is estimated to possess approximately 30 percent of the world's known cobalt reserves, and produces over 50 percent of the world output, while Zambia, its neighbor to the south, possesses an additional 16 percent of the world's known cobalt reserves and contributes an additional 10 percent of the world output.[25] Zaire is also an important source of industrial diamonds, accounting for fully 39 percent of the world output.[26] In recent years Nigeria has been a major supplier of U.S. petroleum imports; ranking as the seventh largest oil producer in the world, Nigeria provides 18 percent of U.S. crude petroleum imports, making it second only to Saudi Arabia as a supplier to the U.S. market.[27] Finally, manganese—a mineral essential to the production of almost all steels—is found largely in Africa south of the Sahara and in the USSR. Currently South Africa produces about a quarter of the world's manganese, while the largest producer in Black Africa is Gabon, which accounts for 9 percent of world production. The U.S. must import virtually all its manganese needs, and it relies on Gabon for about one-third and South Africa for approximately one-tenth of its supply.[28] The strategic significance of manganese is open to question, however, since the enormous quantities of the material on the ocean floor may reduce the critical importance of supply from resources subject to sovereign control.

This brief review would seem to indicate beyond any doubt that the complementarity between the essential ingredients of modern industrial production, on the one hand, and the unusual mineral endowment of sub-Saharan Africa, on the other, creates a very real U.S. national interest in maintaining continuous and secure access to African minerals. Moreover, since the flow of minerals depends upon the continuous development of reserves, it is also necessary, from the Western point of view, that there be a continuous application of capital and technology to at least certain sectors of Africa's mining industry. Thus what we earlier concluded was a private economic interest—i.e., continued access for investment purposes—turns out to embody indirectly a national interest.

Policy Implications of Economic Interests. That the United States has a national interest in continued African production of essential minerals, and in access to that production, would seem to be relatively unambiguous. Less clear, however, are the policy implications of this fact. The acknowledgment of this economically strategic interest usually functions as the linchpin in the argument that the United States must prevent the radical transformation of the political systems which control the supply of critical materials—*especially* when that transformation takes place with Soviet assistance. In general, observers who adopt a radical perspective share this contention with those who adopt conventional views, although their attitude toward the "threat" to U.S. interests will vary. The contention is based upon a logic which assumes that radical governments are likely to deny essential materials to the West—either because they will adopt economic strategies which seek to break their ties to the capitalist economies and/or because they will use their resources as a political weapon, usually in collaboration with or at the behest of the Soviet Union, in order to undermine the Western political economy. Thus persons of every ideological persuasion generally accept the proposition that the rise to power of a radical African regime in South Africa would place in jeopardy the West's access to that country's minerals, and therefore accept the notion that it is in the interests of the United States to foster political stability in the area. Some liberals, agreeing that the United States has important economic interests in South Africa, but unwilling either to call for support of the status quo or accept a loss of these interests in the future, call for strong efforts to undermine the present South African system so as to ingratiate the United States with the African government that would hypothetically come to power there.

It is my contention that all of these perspectives on an appropriate policy are erroneous because they are based on a fallacious proposition—that radical political transformation in Africa will jeopardize the West's access to essential minerals. Despite its nearly universal acceptance, neither logic nor experience supports such a notion. Let us examine the situation with regard to the most important case in economically strategic terms—that of South Africa—and let us assume the "worst," i.e., that a radical movement backed by the Soviet Union will take power from the present minority government.

One of the primary and fundamental structural aspects of the South African economic system is the production of minerals for export. The mining sector is significant not only in terms of its contribution to GNP (contributing approximately 13 percent) and employment, but also because the export of a large proportion of its product earns the necessary foreign reserve to finance the essential importation of technology and of industrial and consumer goods. No South African government, however radical, could afford to forego the revenue earned by mineral exports, and the only significant market for South African minerals is the U.S. and its allies.* Thus any government in power in South Africa, whatever its ideological coloration, would be locked into selling its industrial raw materials to the West just as the West is locked into buying them. Ironically, this would be *especially* true for a radical African regime, which would, one must assume, attempt to satisfy the social welfare demands of the population to a greater degree than the present minority government. The resources to pay an enlarged welfare bill—for education, health facilities, housing, and the like—would have to come out of overall economic expansion, and given the nature of the South African economy such an expansion would entail as one of its crucial elements an increase in export earnings. Thus a radical regime in South Africa, interested in increasing its foreign reserve flow, would be motivated to *expand* the export of its minerals and not the reverse, as is suggested by the conventional wisdom on the subject. This has implications for government policy in the area of foreign capital and technology as well. The domestic need to increase mineral export earnings and thus to maintain and even increase mining production, combined with

---

*Gold dominates the South African mining sector with respect to contribution to GNP, employment, and revenue earned. However, for over a decade the relative position of non-gold mining in all of these categories has been steadily decreasing (see Republic of South Africa, Department of Statistics, *South African Statistics* [annual]).

the need to expand overall industrial production as a basis for increasing welfare and employment, would place a radical regime in South Africa in the position of seeking external capital, technology, and management resources. Even the present economic system, controlled by the dominant minority, relies heavily on external capital and technology. How much more reliant would a new regime be—having to answer to a much larger support base and therefore more earnestly in need of economic expansion? This external dependence would be not only for capital technology, but also for management and technical know-how, as a black government sought to remove economic control from the old dominant minority. Since the Soviet Union demonstrates neither the capability nor willingness to take on the task of subsidizing an economy like South Africa's (as it has the less developed and less sophisticated Cuban economy), there would be simply no alternative open to a new government of South Africa but to turn to the West for the supply of needed capital, technology, and management.

The above argument applies with equal—if not greater—force to the countries north of the Zambezi that have economic significance for the U.S. The economies of Zaire, Zambia, and Nigeria are all structurally centered around the extraction and export of minerals. In Zambia, the mining sector accounts for 40 percent of GNP, 90 percent of export earnings, and 54 percent of government revenues.* In Zaire the comparable figures are 24 percent, 81 percent, and 29 percent.[29] Oil plays a similar role in the contemporary Nigerian economy, accounting for 45 percent of GNP, 94 percent of export earnings, and 80 percent of government revenue.†[30] Given this situation, and given the development and welfare goals pursued by African governments, there is simply no way that these African states can forego selling their minerals abroad. And the only substantial customers available are found in the industrial West.** It is

---

*See Barclay Bank Group, *Country Reports*, 2 December 1975. Since 1974 the mining sector has played a smaller role in Zambia as a consequence of the drastic fall in world copper prices. This does not undermine the point being made, however, since an attendant consequence of the reduced export earnings has been economic collapse.

†The contribution of petroleum to GNP in Nigeria has risen extremely rapidly during the 1970's. In 1967/68 the mining sector, including oil, contributed 6 percent to GNP, and in 1973/74 the figure was 16 percent; in 1976/77 oil alone contributed 45 percent.

**As of the end of 1977, for example, fully 55 percent of Nigeria's petroleum exports were destined for the U.S. (see *U.S. News and World Report*, December 5, 1977).

true that radical governments would be likely to pursue an economic strategy whose goal would be economic diversification, and thus less overall reliance on the minerals-export sector, but this would entail a decline in mineral exports *relative* to other economic sectors—not an absolute decline. Indeed the very goal of diversification implies a continuation and even expansion (in absolute terms) of mineral exports, since only from this sector can the capital and foreign reserve necessary to finance new economic activity be generated.

We need not rest the case regarding the compatibility of African radicalism and Western economic interests on the structural logic presented above. An examination of the policies adopted by radical African governments reveals the empirical reality of this logic and thus further exposes the spuriousness of an automatic linkage between radicalism and the secession of economic intercourse with the West. Congo/Brazzaville and Benin are the states in Africa making the most vociferous claims to be following the course of Marxism-Leninism and "Scientific Socialism." Despite a constant stream of invective against international capitalist penetration, the governments of both these countries have permitted French public and private interests to maintain a dominant role in their economies, and have continuously sought to assuage the fears of private investors. Thus in 1975 the Congolese government reassured private capital that the "Congo was wide open to foreign trade and investment."[31] And in a statement that could as well have been made about Benin, a respected source on African affairs notes of Congo/Brazzaville: "Socialism has made little difference . . . to the country's economy, which remains largely under the control of the French interests."[32]

It might be argued that given their small size and meager resources, the experiences of Benin and Congo/Brazzaville are not particularly instructive or generalizable. However, if we turn to other candidates for "radical" status in sub-Saharan Africa—states with more substantial political resources and economic potential—the picture is not substantially different, although the rhetorical attacks directed at Western capitalism are far less in evidence. Guinea, under the leadership of Sékou Touré, is the sub-Saharan African state with the longest continuous record of radicalism and strained political relations with the West. It is also the state in the region with the closest long-standing relationship with the Soviet Union—a relationship made manifest by, among other things, its making Guinean airfields available to the Soviets for military reconnaissance flights over the South Atlantic, and its allowing the use of Guinean refueling facilities by Soviet ships ferrying men and material to aid the MPLA cause in Angola.³³ This close political relationship with the Soviets, however, has not precluded Guinea's having significant business ties with the West.

Guinea's main economic resource is bauxite. Either in its natural state or refined into alumina, bauxite accounts for 95 percent of Guinean export earnings. Guinea possesses approximately two-thirds of the world's known deposits, and its current development plan aims at making the country the world's largest bauxite exporter.³⁴ Western countries and multinational corporations are heavily involved in this crucial sector of the Guinean economy—both as customers for its bauxite and alumina and as suppliers of capital, technology, and management. The economies of the industrial West continue to dominate Guinean exports, with the proportion of export earnings accounted for by purchases from the EEC and the United States being twice that from sales to Comecon.* Two companies in which foreign multinationals play a central role dominate the minerals sector of the Guinean economy: the Compagnie des Bauxites de Guinée, which mines the large bauxite deposits at Boké in the northwestern part of the country, and Friguia, which both mines bauxite and refines a portion of it into alumina. Each operation is a joint venture between a consortium of Western corporations and the government of Guinea, in which the foreign component is the majority shareholder (51 percent).³⁵ Through their participation in one or both of these ventures, a number of the major mining multinationals have made sizable investments in postcolonial Guinea—Alcoa (U.S.), Pechiney-Ugine (France), Noranda Mines Ltd. (Canada), Alcan (Canada), British Aluminium Co. (U.K.), Vereinigte Aluminium-Werke (Germany), and Schweizerische Aluminium AG (Switzerland).³⁶ There are other examples of significant Western participation in Guinea's mining sector as well. In 1971 the Swiss firm Schweizerische Aluminium entered into an agreement with the government of Guinea to establish a joint-venture company (50:50) for the exploration of major bauxite deposits in the Fouta-Djalon region. The agreement is to run for a period of seventy-five years.³⁷ Another example is the Compagnie Francaise des Pétroles, which has a 20 percent stake in SOGIP, the Guinean state-corporation engaged in offshore oil exploration.³⁸ Foreign business is also

---

*See Legum, ed., *Africa Contemporary Record*, 1975/76, p. B707. In recent years Guinea's trade with the West has dramatically increased and that with the planned economies has undergone a corresponding decline. Thus in 1973 Comecon accounted for 25 percent of Guinea's total imports, but by 1975 this figure was down to 11 percent, with expectations for a still further decline.

found in the small Guinean manufacturing sector. There is, for example, an American truck-assembly plant, a British textile factory, and a Franco-Spanish clinker plant.[39] In sum, the close political ties that Guinea has developed with the Soviet Union have not affected its willingness to sell its minerals to the West, nor have these political ties led to an end to business and investment activity by Western firms within Guinea.

A similar situation obtains in Angola and Mozambique. While continuing to rely on Soviet and Cuban military, technical, and economic assistance, the Angolan government has emphatically pursued a policy of economic nonalignment. During 1976 it reached an agreement with Gulf Oil for the resumption of production in the Cabinda oil fields. By the beginning of 1977 the production of this U.S. firm accounted for 80 percent of Angola's export earnings, and its tax and royalty payments accounted for the majority of government revenue (estimates vary from 50 to 90 percent).[40] The Gulf facility is operated by a sixty-man expatriate staff which is, ironically, protected from local Cabinda "nationalist" insurgents by a contingent of Cuban troops.[41] The relationship worked out between the Neto regime and Gulf Oil is not an isolated instance, but rather an important aspect of a larger pragmatic policy orientation. While nationalizing the banks and the Portuguese companies that were abandoned by their owners during and immediately after the 1975 civil war, the Angolan government has repeatedly stated its willingness to permit established foreign-owned companies to continue operations as well as to welcome new foreign investors. Thus on 14 February 1976 Eduardo dos Santos, the Angolan Foreign Minister, made the following statement:

> We are ready to respect the interests of the multinational companies in Angola if they aid the development of our country and are benefit to our people. . . . As a general rule, we have no intention at the moment of proceeding with nationalizations, except for those foreign, commercial and industrial enterprises that have been abandoned by their owners.[42]

Within this policy framework, arrangements have been worked out with a variety of Western multinationals in addition to Gulf—e.g., Texaco, Petrofina, Fiat, Volvo, and deBeers—and negotiations are under way with a host of other foreign firms regarding new investment opportunities.[43]

The situation in Mozambique parallels that of Angola. David Ottaway reports that "far from pushing the rapid . . . nationalization of the the tottering private sector, [the Mozambique] government is actively courting the remaining private owners to keep their factories open."[44] Nationalization has occurred in the banking, insurance, and oil distribution sectors, but the Frelimo government has stressed that it does not intend to carry out a blanket nationalization program, and indeed has taken pains to guarantee an important place for foreign, private investment.[45] President Machel has made two major overseas tours to Western countries to improve economic relations. One of these was to the United States and provided an opportunity for the Mozambican Minister of Industry to hold a discussion with several American businessmen on investment opportunities. As a concrete step to encourage foreign investors, the Maputo regime lifted a ban on profit repatriation that had been imposed by the Portuguese in 1972.[46] The openness of the Mozambique government to foreign business is also reflected in a number of recent corporate ventures: General Tire International, a U.S. firm, opened a factory during 1977; Hunt Petroleum of the U.S. announced that it would resume oil prospecting; the Companhia Carbonifeira de Mocambique, a Belgian-owned firm, continued to mine the country's major coal deposits; and a Swedish company—LKAB International—announced that it would start prospecting for iron ore deposits, which the government hopes one day will become the basis for a steel industry.[47]

If close relations by African states with the USSR portend an economic war with the West, then this should be revealed in the policies followed by Guinea, Angola, and Mozambique. The governments of all three countries owe their rise to power and/or their initial survival after independence in large part to Soviet aid, and all three states have political relations with the USSR that are the closest of any country in sub-Saharan Africa. An examination of the economic policy of these states reveals, however, that the conventional equation between radicalism and Soviet influence on the one hand, and a threat to Western economic interests on the other, is misguided. Indeed the policies followed vis-à-vis foreign investments are similar to, and may well be more liberal than, those adopted by many African states usually thought of as "moderate" (e.g., Nigeria, Zambia, Ghana, Sierra Leone, and the like).

The argument that the U.S. must prevent the destabilization and radicalization of African political systems if it is to protect vital economic interests is rendered dubious not only by the structural and empirical analysis provided above, but also by the altered pattern of international business activity over the past decade, which

U.S. ECONOMIC INTERESTS: POLICY IMPLICATIONS

has rendered obsolete the simple equation between radical governments, nationalization, and damaged U.S. economic interests. To begin with, the phenomenon of nationalization is no longer peculiar to radical governments. The economic nationalism that has characterized even the most conservative and pro-Western governments (Iran and Saudi Arabia, for instance) has produced widespread efforts to gain indigenous control over the subsidiaries of multinational corporations. In sub-Saharan Africa such "moderate" governments as exist in contemporary Nigeria and Zambia have led the way in placing increasing strictures on foreign business activity and in forcing international companies to sell ever larger shares of their local operations to either private citizens or the state. Indeed, as we noted above, in some respects these "moderates" deal more harshly with the multinational investor than the "radical" governments in Angola, Guinea, and Mozambique.* Except in the highest technology industries, the era of the wholly-owned foreign subsidiary may be drawing to a close. This has not, however, meant an end to the international operations of U.S. firms. Rather the MNCs have adapted to the political realities of the 1970's and modified their economic activities accordingly, generating earnings through licensing their technology, entering management and sales contracts, selling equipment and intermediate goods, and providing loan capital, rather than through the ownership and control of subsidiaries operating on foreign soil.

An ironic counterpart to the growing hostility of "moderate" governments toward foreign ownership of local business, and the resultant modification of business practices by MNCs, has been the emerging cooperative relationship between U.S. businesses and Communist governments. With the issue of ownership no longer in contention, the governments of countries like the USSR, China, Vietnam, and Cuba have been desirous of obtaining access to Western, and especially U.S., capital and technology. U.S. corporations give every indication of wishing to reciprocate this interest, and it is the U.S. government, not the hostility of Communist governments to Western capitalism, that has hampered the emerging relationship. From the perspective of the MNCs, once ownership and control of subsidiaries is no longer the prerequisite for doing business, the

---

*While foreign oil companies in Nigeria were forced to sell 60 percent of their equity to the government, and mining firms in Zambia were completely taken over by the state, Gulf Oil was permitted to retain 45 percent ownership in its Angolan subsidiary, and in Guinea the foreign multinationals have majority control of the two largest mining operations in the country.

most important single concern is the confidence they can have that host governments will not unilaterally alter the terms of the contracts they have entered into. On this score, the track record of "moderate" governments, who are often attracted to economic nationalism as a device to mobilize short-term popular support, is not very impressive.[48] For a company generating foreign earnings from management contracts, technology licenses, and equipment sales, a firmly rooted Marxist-Leninist government may be a better business risk. Thus have the changing politics of the countries of the third world and the concomitant modifications in tne operations of international business turned the world of the 1950's on its head.

To summarize then, the structure of the African economies, the related content of government policy, and the changing nature of the relations between international firms and host governments, whatever their ideological leanings, all undercut the notion that the U.S. must prevent the emergence of radical regimes in order to protect its economic interests. To be sure, a fundamental transformation in a country's political arrangements might well create a transitional period of reduced mineral production, but a farsighted program of Western stockpiling, some of which already occurs, could meet this difficulty.* Stockpiling would also be an effective counter to any government, in the present or future, that sought to use its mineral resources for political ends through the use of boycotts. This is, of course, a common worst-case scenario in security discussions. In order for it to be an effective weapon, a boycott's effects must be rapidly felt in the importing country. Stockpiling allows such a country to buffer itself for a period of several years from the effects of resource denial, during which time the country doing the boycotting suffers the loss of export revenues. In the African case, where governments rely on export earnings to pay for vital imports, the political costs of sustaining a boycott would be felt particularly rapidly and acutely, at the very same time that its benefits would be nil. In such a situation the idea that a government in, say, Nigeria would or could withhold its oil from the United States—or Zaire withhold its cobalt and diamonds—is utterly implausible.†

---

*The Critical Materials Stockpiling Act of 1946 provides the authority for government stockpiles in the United States. In 1976 the President approved new stockpile policy guidelines. The new policy calls for stockpiles of critical materials to cover three years' use (see U.S. Department of Interior, *Mining and Minerals Policy* 1977, p. 26).

†The spectre of mineral "hold-ups" is not raised only in discussions within

U.S. ECONOMIC INTERESTS: POLICY IMPLICATIONS

The generally accepted view on recent developments in the Horn of Africa, in southern Africa, and in Zaire has been that radicalization, particularly when it is aided by the Soviet Union, is a threat to the tangible interests of the United States in the sub-Saharan Africa region. Careful analysis has revealed, however, that this commonly held view is fundamentally erroneous. Neither the military-strategic position of the United States nor its economic system would likely be adversely affected even in the event of radical victories in Rhodesia, South Africa, Zaire, and the Horn. There are no significant U.S. military interests in the region, and the very real and vital economic interests that do exist are such as to defy a simple inverse correlation between radicalization and the welfare of the United States.

The conventional notion that radical solutions necessarily mean a threat to the United States has a variety of unfortunate effects: it locks the United States into an antagonistic, or extremely tentative, posture toward movements of oppressed groups; it produces a supportive posture toward admittedly unsavory political regimes; and it has often led to an interventionist stance in situations in which no national interests are at stake. The Zaire crisis of June 1978, which will be dealt with later, is the most recent example of this phenomenon. A clearer understanding of U.S. interests in the African region, and how they would be affected by radical political change (and Cuban/Soviet involvement), should help free policy from an automatically negative orientation toward such developments, and open the option of a "non-involved" policy posture, even in the face of apparent increases in Soviet involvement. However, this would be so only if policy were shaped by a concern for protecting and furthering tangible interests. Recent U.S. policy in Africa reveals that in the thinking of many important policymakers this concern is only a part—indeed a secondary part—of the overall picture that must be considered.

the national security community. Proponents of strong U.S. action against the minority regime in South Africa often point out that Nigeria is the chief non-Arab supplier of U.S. petroleum imports, and that by offending Nigeria with a weak southern Africa policy the United States is jeopardizing these oil supplies. For the reasons noted above, however, this proposition should be considered little more than political rhetoric. While the United States may now depend on Nigeria for a significant portion (18 percent) of its oil imports, Nigeria sells about half of its petroleum to the U.S. market. Since revenue from oil sales to the United States makes up a major share of government revenue, and since, despite its oil boom, Nigeria is unable to sell enough oil to cover its planned expenditures, a boycott of the U.S. market would be suicidal—it would hurt Nigeria far more than the United States.

III

GLOBAL CONSIDERATIONS IN AFRICA POLICY

In the view of the Secretary of State during the two previous administrations, and of the current adviser on National Security Affairs to President Carter, considerations of global strategy (the responsibility of the United States as a Great Power) should take precedence over more narrowly conceived "regional" interests. While usually consistent with each other, the two types of "interests"—global and regional—are in the short term not necessarily identical. The most explicit statement of this differentiation in the African case was made by Secretary of State Kissinger when he argued for an activist role for the United States in the Angolan civil war before the Senate Foreign Relations Committee:

> America's modest direct strategic and economic interests in Angola are not the central issue. *The question is whether America maintains the resolve to act responsibly as a great power.* . . . The culprits in the tragedy that is now unfolding in Angola are the Soviet Union and its client state, Cuba. But I must note . . . that the Executive has been deprived of indispensable flexibility in formulating a foreign policy which we believe to be in our national interest. . . . *A stable relationship with the Soviet Union based on mutual restraint will be achieved only if Soviet lack of restraint carries the risk of counteraction. The consequences [of inaction] may well be far-reaching and substantially more painful than the course we have recommended.*[49]

This statement was made in January 1976 in reference to Angola, but its echo continues to be heard in the statements of Carter administration spokesmen, who even more intensely than Kissinger speak of the need to counter the Cubans and Soviets in Africa for the sake of global considerations. In the final analysis the case for a U.S. interventionist role in sub-Saharan Africa does not rest on the significance of tangible interests there, although such interests and a threat to them are assumed to exist from increased Soviet/Cuban activity, but rather on the need to maintain the image of U.S. resolve and determination. What can be observed here is the specific operationalization of the foreign policy paradigm which has dominated U.S. actions since the late 1950's—a paradigm based on the theory of limited war and distilled into what Jonathan Schell has termed the "Doctrine of Credibility."[50]

The theory of limited war was developed in order to provide a strategic doctrine which could attain two vital but apparently contradictory goals: on the one hand, prevent global Communist rule through the spread of Soviet influence and power, and on the other, prevent the extinction of the world in a nuclear war. Once the assumption is made that the Soviet Union is committed to a policy of dominating the U.S., and the West in general, the fact that the USSR is capable of launching a major nuclear attack creates a very fundamental and special kind of dilemma for U.S. policymakers. In the words of Henry Kissinger, a major architect of limited war doctrine, "the enormity of modern weapons makes the thought of war repugnant, but the refusal to run any risks would amount to giving the Soviet rulers a blank check."[51] The doctrine of massive retaliation was hardly suited for such a situation, since the threat to initiate mutual nuclear incineration in situations where immediate survival was not at stake was simply not credible. Indeed, with massive retaliation as the only option, the effectiveness of nuclear deterrence was itself open to question, since there would not be any means available to demonstrate the will of the United States to use its nuclear arsenal should its vital interests be threatened. The United States would have to depend on its enemy believing it had the resolve to initiate mutual suicide without being able to act so as to give it reason to harbor such a belief. The notion of limited war was an answer to both these problems. First, it provided the means to check the spread of Soviet power in peripheral areas without a direct U.S.-Soviet nuclear exchange. More important, by providing an arena for the United States to demonstrate its resolve, its will to act in defense of what it perceived to be the correct world order, the intervention of the United States in peripheral areas constituted a mechanism to sustain the credibility of its deterrent. That is, by denying Soviet leaders a "blank check," the United States could not only stem the spread of Soviet power, but could also put those leaders on notice regarding what would be in store for them should *real* U.S. interests be threatened. Thus General Maxwell Taylor, another architect of limited war doctrine, wrote:

> There is . . . an important psychological factor which must be present to make the retaliatory weapon [the nuclear deterrent force] effective. It must be clear to the aggressor that we have the will and determination to use our retaliatory power without compunction if we are attacked. Any suggestion of weakness or indecision may encourage the enemy to gamble on surprise.[52]

Preparing for, and occasionally fighting, a "limited war" would guard against the danger that "repeated [Communist] success in creeping aggression may encourage a Communist miscalculation that could lead to general war."[53] Throughout the 1960's this concern with demonstrating U.S. resolve, with preventing an erosion of "credibility," was a major theme in U.S. foreign policy.*

Despite some hesitation at the outset of its tenure, and continuing reluctance in some quarters, the Carter administration has seemingly embraced this same credibility doctrine as the cornerstone of its policy toward sub-Saharan Africa. The question that arises is whether or not the credibility doctrine is a reasonable basis for the making of U.S. foreign policy in the last quarter of the twentieth century. An examination of its operation in Africa provides an opportunity to examine this issue.

CREDIBILITY AND POWER

There can be little argument with the notion that "credibility" is an important dimension of power. Whether we are talking about individuals or states, the belief on the part of *alter* that *ego* has the ability to bring unpleasant sanctions to bear should *alter* behave in a manner contrary to *ego's* wishes is likely to have a deterrent

---

*Henry Kissinger's development of the notion of detente with the Soviet Union appeared to many to be a major departure from the Cold War policy paradigm composed of the theory of limited war and the derivative doctrine of credibility. However, to see detente as other than an important tactical addition to the same strategic doctrine is a serious error. Kissinger saw increasing enmeshment between the Soviet and U.S. economies as producing a situation in which dependence by the USSR on American capital and technology would force the Soviet leaders to accept a U.S. definition of the appropriate world order and the Soviet role in it. But this should be viewed as additive to, not as a substitute for, the policy posture of an earlier era. Should economic "realities" be ignored—i.e., should the Soviets play a role in upsetting the international status quo—then direct and forceful action by the U.S. would be necessary to underline the credibility of American world power. This is the clear lesson of Kissinger's recommendations in the Angolan situation, and the message of his statement to the Senate quoted above (p. 30).

effect on such behavior. Moreover, this psychological resource is a far more efficient basis of power from ego's point of view than having to physically prevent alter from engaging in the unwanted behavior. It is also fairly obvious that ego's psychological advantage—its credibility—will diminish to the extent that unwanted behavior by alter is allowed to occur without calling forth the threatened negative sanctions. Note the obvious point that ego's credibility is based *not* on having to respond to all of alter's behavior, but just those acts that have been specified by ego as undesirable.

Now ego's power over alter might well be enhanced in any specific instance if it defined a large number of behaviors—even ones peripheral to its concerns—as prohibited, and brought sanctions to bear when transgressions occurred. An ego willing and able to demonstrate its use of sanctions in matters of only marginal concern should have a particularly formidable psychological edge in those situations it defines as vital. However, this enhanced credibility is achieved at a significant price. For now ego, having cast its net over a wide area, must be ready and able to deliver sanctions in many more situations—i.e., there will be more occasions when its credibility will be placed "on the line." And should ego find that it lacks the resources to cover all these situations, that it is unable to bring sanctions effectively to bear in those areas of only marginal concern, then its psychological edge in matters of vital concern will be eroded. In other words, by defining its area of concern extremely broadly, ego enhances its credibility, and at the same time it renders that credibility more vulnerable to erosion. This paradox is extremely important in the analysis of current U.S. foreign policy and particularly with regard to its current efforts in sub-Saharan Africa.

What must be understood at the outset about the maintenance of U.S. credibility as an international actor is that the situations in which that credibility is tested are not fixed, or given, in some objective sense. They are in part defined by U.S. policymakers and political leaders when they make statements about what is important to their country. U.S. credibility would not be undermined by inaction in a situation in which political leaders made it clear that the country had no important stake. But once a situation is publicly defined as threatening to U.S. interests or, as is increasingly common, as a test of the country's will, determination, and resolve, then a lack of U.S. response might well place in jeopardy the psychological dimension of U.S. power.

Unfortunately, one of the cornerstones of limited war theory and the doctrine of credibility as they have evolved in the past two decades is the completely open-ended definition of the situations that test U.S. determination vis-à-vis the Soviets. Starting with a conception of world politics as essentially a titanic and zero-sum struggle between a Western and Soviet "sphere," any activity of the Soviet Union beyond its prescribed sphere involves ipso facto a corresponding reduction in the "Western" sphere, and thus calls for a credibility-bolstering response. Anything short of this would be offering the Soviets a "blank check." And the existence of nuclear arsenals adds the irony that it is better to bolster credibility in those areas where Soviet involvement is most minimal—i.e., where the risk of direct confrontation would be the least. Note that within this foreign policy paradigm the maintenance of credibility is divorced from the protection of tangible interests. In terms of decisions about the use of American power abroad, the distinction between vital and non-vital interests is obliterated, as are all gradations in-between. Every situation involving Soviet activity demands a successful U.S. blocking action, regardless of whether significant tangible interests are at stake. Indeed, just as situations of minimal Soviet involvement are best suited for demonstrations of U.S. credibility, so the more minimal the U.S. stake in a situation which calls forth action, the more dramatic the message regarding the U.S. will to act.

Whatever U.S. foreign policy success can be attributed to the doctrine of credibility was conditioned by two factors that must be present for it to operate successfully—factors that have ceased to exist in the contemporary world system. The first was the relative military weakness and/or inhibition of the Soviet Union. One of the peculiar features of the "credibility game" as it is structured by limited war theory is that it can be played successfully and safely only when there is a single player. What if Soviet leaders decided to reject the U.S. definition of the proper world order and instead began to project their own vision by demonstrating Soviet credibility wherever they perceived Western behavior, or just some changing political situation, to run counter to this vision? If both nuclear powers based their foreign policy on the notion that their determination needed to be constantly demonstrated in every corner of the globe in order to deny the other side a "blank check," then a direct confrontation—the very situation "credibility bolstering" is supposed to prevent—would seem inevitable. The potential for just such a situation has developed in the post-Vietnam era as the Soviet Union has for the first time emerged alongside the United States as a genuine global power—that is, as a state with the will and military capability to project its power on a global scale. This at least would certainly seem to be the lesson of its current Africa policy.

The second factor allowing for the successful operationalization of the doctrine of credibility was the absence of autonomous power in the Latin American, Asian, and African periphery. Either as a result of economic ties, as in the case of Latin America, or of colonialism, as in Asia and Africa, the United States could for many years pursue demonstrations of its resolve in the "periphery" without very much need to concern itself with the local repercussions of its policy. In the 1970's, however, a more pluralistic world politics may well place regional constraints on the ability of the U.S. to pursue demonstrations of credibility. Under these changed circumstances—a Soviet Union more willing and able to demonstrate *its* resolve, and a periphery less automatically accepting of Western action—the weakness of a foreign policy based primarily upon demonstrating credibility becomes manifest. A completely *open-ended* and publicly stated commitment to a demonstration of resolve under these new circumstances creates expectations which cannot easily be fulfilled, and thus establishes the condition for the very erosion of credibility that it was the purpose of policy to avoid. An examination of current U.S. efforts to counter the Cubans and Soviets in sub-Saharan Africa provides an excellent lesson in the limitation of the credibility doctrine under contemporary circumstances.

U.S. CREDIBILITY AND SOVIET/CUBAN INVOLVEMENT IN AFRICA

We have already seen that the activity of Cuba and the Soviet Union in Africa poses no significant threat to what might be thought of as the tangible interests of the United States. Despite this, the major foreign policy spokesmen of both the Ford and Carter administrations have spared few opportunities to publicly call attention to the "threatening" activity of the Communist powers on the African continent, to demand its secession, and to threaten (at least implicitly) some U.S. response. These public statements have sometimes focused on the "threat" to regional economic or military interests, and they have also explicitly or by implication pictured the Soviet and Cuban involvement in Africa as providing a test of U.S. resolve to shoulder its global responsibilities. The frequent announcement that the United States is being "tested," coupled with the repeated challenge to the Communist powers to cease their activities, would certainly seem to have placed U.S. credibility "on the line" in sub-Saharan Africa. And, it should be noted, the Soviet Union and its allies are not the only audience for this credibility test. As U.S. leaders and various policy analysts have often pointed out, a failure to respond to the Soviets in Africa may weaken the confidence of allies in the ability of the United States to meet its commitments. Furthermore, high-level statements about threatening Soviet moves have repercussions within the American domestic political arena. Once Soviet actions are described as ominous and denounced by administration spokesmen, a failure to do anything effective about them creates an image of weakness for the President, which in turn adversely affects his standing in the polls and thus his future electoral chances.

Having raised the issue of a "test of credibility" over recent Cuban/Soviet activity in sub-Saharan Africa, the Carter administration, and that of Gerald Ford before it, have had great difficulty in performing adequately on their self-proclaimed "test." The reasons for this relate to the changing nature of Soviet power, the character of intra-African political affairs, and the constraints of domestic American politics. This can be seen through the analysis of the four "crises" in sub-Saharan Africa that have drawn the most public attention of the Ford and Carter administrations—Angola, Ethiopia, Rhodesia/Zimbabwe, and Zaire.

Angola and Ethiopia. The direct military commitment that has been made in Angola and Ethiopia by the Communist powers is certainly unprecedented as far as their involvement in sub-Saharan Africa is concerned. Indeed, the presence on the continent of an estimated forty thousand Cuban troops, their participation in actual combat, and the willingness and *capacity* of the Soviet Union to supply them with transport, logistics, and large amounts of even heavy weaponry at very substantial financial cost exceeds any Russian (not to mention Cuban) military intervention outside of Eastern Europe and Korea since World War II.* The lesson that some have drawn from the unprecedented scope and scale of this Communist activity in Africa is that some direct American counter-response—a demonstration of U.S.

---

*In Spring 1978 the Deputy Director of the CIA, Frank Carlucci, told the Senate that Soviet support for Ethiopia's campaigns in the Ogaden and Eritrea included the supply of four hundred tanks, fifty MIGS, and "huge quantities of armored cars, personnel carriers and artillery." The CIA estimated the cost of the Ethiopian operation to the Soviets at one billion dollars (*San Francisco Examiner*, April 10, 1978).

resolve—is especially necessary.* The situation, however, holds another and very different message as well. It is that there is now more than one player in the "credibility game." With the Soviets apparently willing and able to play a role as a global power, the stakes involved in demonstrating resolve through military means in situations in which the Russians are already deeply involved are far higher than they were previously. Thus a direct military involvement by the United States in Angola and Ethiopia entails a commitment of substantial magnitude, and also contains a significant risk of direct confrontation with the Soviet Union. Under these circumstances not only is the cost-effectiveness of the "credibility doctrine" seriously eroded, but, more importantly, the basis of the doctrine's persuasiveness evaporates as the very demonstration of credibility provides the catalyst for that which it was intended to prevent—direct superpower confrontation.

Ironically, at the very time that demonstrations of credibility involve an increase in the scale of necessary commitments, the American public, especially as it is made manifest through its representatives in Congress, has become reluctant to support the use of *any* resources for direct intervention in "peripheral" areas. The refusal of Congress to permit the Ford administration to expand its covert operations in Angola, despite strong backing for such a policy by Secretary Kissinger, was a dramatic testimonial to this new reality in domestic American politics. This poses an acute dilemma for any incumbent President, since the reluctance of Congress to support foreign intervention does not relieve him of the public's expectation that "threatening" Soviet behavior should be countered and stopped by the United States. Thus a President concerned about his domestic standing ought to be especially careful about publicly defining situations as threatening and as tests of U.S. resolve. If he chooses to raise the public alarm over situations which he is unable to affect, he will himself have helped create the circumstances that produce his image of weakness. In other words,

---

*Thus Zbigniew Brzezinski told NBC's "Meet the Press" on May 28, 1978: "I do not believe that this kind of Soviet-Cuban involvement ought to be cost free and there are a variety of ways in which concerned countries can convince [them] that their involvement, their intrusion, is not only conducive to greater international instability, but in fact carries with it consequences which may be inimical to them as well." Earlier Brzezinski was widely reported to have favored extensive U.S. military aid to Somalia as a counter to Soviet/Cuban assistance to Ethiopia. See Jan Austin and Banning Garrett, "U.S. Africa Policy: Hardening the Line," *International Bulletin* 5, 11 (June 5, 1978), p. 5.

in circumstances in which an interventionist foreign policy is subject to severe constraint, it is corrosive to a President's domestic political support to espouse, and operate under, a doctrine which holds that essentially all Soviet activity outside of its USSR-Eastern European sphere creates the basis for a test of U.S. resolve. As a general rule, tests that one has a poor chance of passing ought to be avoided, not created.

The difficulties that the U.S. administration has had in fashioning a direct response to Soviet and Cuban activity in Africa are not restricted to the new assertiveness and capacity of these Communist states, or the post-Vietnam domestic constraint on an interventionist foreign policy. The way in which the Soviet/Cuban involvement fits into the dynamics of African regional politics has also presented a major obstacle to designing a wholly satisfying response. The simple fact is that the United States has had preciously little success in finding support among African states for its perception of the negative role that Cuban troops and their Soviet advisors and suppliers have been playing in Ethiopia and in Angola. What the United States chooses to call aggression, intervention, and destabilization has been accorded a significant modicum of legitimacy by many African states.* When President Carter, in his major speech during the recent state visit to Nigeria, devoted a central portion of his attention to decrying the Soviet and Cuban intervention in Africa, his remarks were met with little enthusiasm, if not a degree of hostility. Some observers have chosen to explain this divergence in African and U.S. perception by pointing to the fact that in Ethiopia and in Angola the Cubans and Soviets are present on the invitation of established and internationally recognized governments. Moreover, the fact that France, under similar invitation, has for years had several thousand troops permanently stationed in over a dozen sub-Saharan African countries, that it used its military in Gabon during the 1960's, and that it is currently engaged in military actions in Chad and the Western Sahara, coupled with the fact that the United States has not opposed this French activity, has given a hollow, if

---

*Thus the Foreign Minister of Kenya, regarded as one of the most pro-Western African countries, told a foreign journalist: "The Cubans have changed the history of Africa. On the question of racial subjugation in southern Africa, no one can convince me that the Azanians, Zimbabweans, and Namibians should not get assistance from elsewhere if they are denied assistance by the West. . . . Were it not for the assistance of the Cubans and the Soviets the Ethiopian army might easily have been defeated by Somalia. If Kenya were in a similar position and no one wanted to assist us, and the Cubans agreed to help us, do you think Kenya would refuse?" (*To the Point* 5, 32 [August 11, 1978], p. 24).

not hypocritical, ring to the concerned statements of U.S. spokesmen about the dangers of foreign intervention.* The "legal" basis to the Soviet/Cuban presence and the inconsistency in the U.S. position on foreign intervention in Africa are not, however, the main reasons why African hostility to the Cuban/Soviet involvement in Ethiopia and Angola has been far less than the United States would have wished. The really important point is that the Communist states' involvement has thus far not occurred indiscriminately, but rather only in those situations in which their actions would be supportive of principles that have strong support among the governments of African countries.

In the intra-regional politics of the last two decades two issues have emerged upon which there is an overwhelming consensus, if not unanimity, among the states south of the Sahara—the sacrosanct nature of colonially inherited borders, and the need to eliminate colonial rule (or political control by a settler European minority). That these should be the only two issues that can unite an Organization of African Unity otherwise deeply and complexly divided is not surprising. The common history of colonial domination and racial rule provides the emotional and symbolic significance to the goal of ending white minority rule in southern Africa; and the fact that all African states inherited borders that are culturally and geographically artificial, and that therefore all African governing elites feel vulnerable to potential secession and irredentism, has imbued established borders with a kind of sanctity in the policies adopted by the official strata. The success that the Soviets and Cubans have had in gaining acceptance within the region for their recent large-scale involvement is based on the fact that their actions have been in support of these two principles. In Ethiopia they have aided an African government in resisting two secessionist movements, one

---

*There are an estimated eight thousand French army troops stationed in Africa south of the Sahara. The bulk of these are in Djibouti, Chad, Senegal, Gabon, and the Ivory Coast, with smaller contingents in Cameroon, Mauritania, Togo and Niger. In February 1964 French paratroopers landed in Libreville, capital of Gabon, to reinstate President Leon Mba, who had been ousted in a coup d'etat some forty-two hours earlier. In Chad, French paratroopers, marines, legionnaires, aircraft, and armored cars have been used to back the government in its fight against the Frolinat rebels. Direct intervention occurred in 1968, 1969, and again in April 1978. In May 1978 France intervened on behalf of Mauritania in its conflict with the Polisario, a movement seeking to "liberate" the Western Sahara from the control of Morocco and Mauritania. See "A Diary of Foreign Troops," *New African*, 131 (July 1978), pp. 23-24; and in the same issue, "France Bids to Turn the Colonial Clock Back," pp. 25-26.

of which was supported by an invasion from an ethnically related neighboring country. In Angola, once the Republic of South Africa had intervened militarily on behalf of one side in what previously had been seen as an intra-African civil war, its actions were largely viewed within the continent as helping to prevent a continuation of white rule after the Portuguese departure. Thus the Nigerian head of state, speaking before his fellow heads of state and government at the annual Organization of African Unity meeting, declared that the Russians "were invited into Africa for a purpose," and in every case of Cuban involvement "they intervened as a consequence of failure of Western policies and on behalf of legitimate African interests."[54]

Two things would seem to follow from the above analysis. First, should the Soviets in the future become involved in situations where the sanctity of borders or the continuation of white rule are not at stake, they will be in a diplomatically much less advantageous position within the region. Significantly, General Obasanjo of Nigeria, when he made the statement quoted above praising the Russian and Cuban activity in Africa, added the following: "To the Soviets and their friends, I should like to say that, having been invited to Africa in order to assist in the liberation struggle and the consolidation of national independence, they should not overstay their welcome.[55] Second, for the United States to have demonstrated its resolve by countering the Soviets in Angola or Ethiopia would have meant the use of U.S. power for, what would be perceived in the region, as the preservation of white minority rule and the dismemberment of an established state. The normative implications of such action aside, it would have meant a diplomatic disaster for the United States in Africa, and probably the "third world" generally. While the goodwill of such states may not be necessary to the military or economic survival of the United States, their cooperation in a myriad of international forums is a significant element in the ability of the United States to conduct a successful foreign policy. Being no longer able to propose and dispose in such world bodies as the United Nations and the World Bank, and enmeshed in a variety of negotiations concerning "North-South" relations and the shape of a "new international economic order," U.S. policymakers can hardly view with equanimity an embittered bloc of African nations. Likewise, the development of anti-American sentiment by African governments could be costly to U.S. business, since these governments could discriminate in favor of European and Japanese multinational companies with whom American firms are in competition.

U.S. CREDIBILITY: RHODESIA/ZIMBABWE

To directly counter the Soviet/Cuban involvement in Ethiopia and Angola, then, would have entailed a sacrifice of significant diplomatic interests in the region. If to this cost is added the constraints on action applied by the enhanced capacity of the Soviets and the reluctance of the U.S. public to support foreign military involvement, it can be seen that these were not opportune situations to demonstrate U.S. will. Since tangible interests were not at stake, there was no particular reason for the Carter administration to react to Soviet moves as if they were directed against the United States, and to make these the centerpiece of its foreign policy posture. By so doing, the Carter administration created a test of credibility which it was not prepared to win, and thus by its own definition of the situation may have done more to undermine U.S. credibility with adversaries and allies, as well as the credibility of the President with the American public, than anything the Soviets have done on their own.

Rhodesia/Zimbabwe. The foregoing analysis of the Angolan and Ethiopian situations and of the general limitations of the doctrine of credibility under contemporary circumstances holds important lessons for two other current "trouble spots" in sub-Saharan Africa—Rhodesia/Zimbabwe and Zaire. From the Spring of 1976, when then Secretary of State Henry Kissinger thrust himself directly into the conflict over the future of Rhodesia, U.S. policy toward the evolving crisis in that country has been essentially reactive, motivated primarily by fears of potential Soviet "gains" rather than by assessments of the actual situation and its impact on tangible U.S. national interests. As was noted at the outset of this essay, Kissinger perceived an analogy between Rhodesia and Angola, where a Soviet/Cuban-backed nationalist group had emerged triumphant. The Angola affair held two lessons for Kissinger. First, it presented a process of escalating violence, increased radicalization, and Soviet domination which could be projected on to the future in Rhodesia. Second, it demonstrated that in the immediate post-Vietnam era the Congress could not be counted on to support, indeed it was likely to sabotage, the use of force by the United States abroad, even when such use was directed at countering the expansion of Soviet influence.* Since the Congress would not allow a forceful response to the Soviet Union in southern Africa, a way

---

*That these two lessons were directly applied to the Rhodesian situation by Secretary Kissinger can be clearly seen in his testimony to the Senate quoted on pages 2 and 30 of this essay.

was sought that would halt the development of the trends in Rhodesia that would call for such a response. Thus was born the strategy of "moderate solution." If the United States could use its influence to simultaneously end the guerrilla insurgency and displace the white minority regime, replacing it with a government based on majority rule, then the Soviet Union, denied the opportunity for intervention created by insurgent violence, would not need to be countered by the United States. In other words, "global stability" could be maintained by *preventing* a test of U.S. credibility in Rhodesia. Thus U.S. policy became tied to a particular kind of solution out of fear of the advantage that would be gained by the Soviets from its alternative. Although developed by Kissinger, this policy has been carried forward by the Carter administration under the rubric of the "Anglo-American Plan."*

However audacious and elegant the "moderate solution" strategy may appear, it is seriously flawed. Its major weakness stems from the fact that the *primary* purpose for which it was developed was to maintain stability in U.S.-USSR global relations, rather than to provide a solution to the Rhodesian crisis. As such its appropriateness to the complexity of that crisis, and its resultant feasibility as a strategy, can be seriously questioned. In the abstract, few could disapprove of the solution for Rhodesia that the Carter administration claims to be working toward—a negotiated settlement among all the parties that would "end the violence," usher in a regime characterized by majority rule and minority rights, and create the conditions for all citizens to work for economic prosperity within the context of political and social stability. In the context of the hard realities of the Rhodesian/Zimbabwe situation, however, such a solution seems dangerously utopian as the basis for U.S. policy. Two things, in particular, undermine any realistic prospect of implementing this solution. First, the very nature of the issues at stake and their lack of amenability to compromise; and second, the lengthy history of bitter personal/political rivalry among the African nationalist groups.

In alluding to what is believed to be the basis for a negotiated settlement, Carter administration spokesmen are fond of using the phrase "majority rule with minority rights." Perhaps nothing captures the element of utopian fantasy in the thinking of this administration better than this juxtaposition. What are "minority rights"?

Within the tradition of American liberalism, the phrase "major-

---

*See discussion on pages 3 and 4 above.

ity rule with minority rights" brings to mind the principle of legal protection of various civil liberties. But in the context of Rhodesia's political conflict, "minority rights" take on a quite different meaning. The concern of highest salience for the southern African white minority is not freedom of speech, assembly, and the like, but what they call their "future security." *The minority rights that are relevant in the current Rhodesia/Zimbabwe crises involve guarantees of this security.* From 1924 onward the European minority of Rhodesia, constituting less than 5 percent of the territory's population, used its virtual monopoly of the franchise to fashion government policy in a way which created for itself a position of economic and social privilege.* Today this minority correctly understands that majority rule, by threatening its control over the governmental apparatus, is tantamount to undermining its social and economic position as well. *Any* African government, especially in the highly mobilized and politicized contemporary situation, can be expected to pursue policies of economic redistribution (in regard to land, particularly), of Africanization in hiring and promotion (what in the United States is called affirmative action), of compensatory government spending in areas of health care, education, rural development, and the like, and of social desegregation. Such policies would be a direct threat to the European minority's "way of life," and thus its representatives are unlikely to negotiate away political control in the absence of guarantees regarding the security of income, property, careers, and social life. *The "rights" that the European minority cares about, those that are particularly salient in contemporary Rhodesia, are thus those of property, job tenure, and social exclusivity.*

On normative grounds one might well ask why the United States is engaged in trying to guarantee the privileged position of a

---

*This is clearly evident in the manner in which governmentally controlled resources are allocated. Thus, until a few months ago, half of Rhodesia's land was legally reserved for ownership by the European minority that constituted less than 5 percent of the population. The European land happened also to be the economically most choice real estate—it contains all the significant urban areas in the country, most of the rail and motor roads, 98 percent of land suitable for afforestation, and 82 percent of land suitable for extensive farming. Distribution of government funds for education is similarly skewed, with the per capita expenditure for African pupils being approximately one-tenth the expenditure for each European child. Government prohibition of African cash crop farming and trade union organization combined with these other disadvantages to create a situation in which 57 percent of total personal income accrues to the less than 5 percent European portion of the population.

small European minority in Africa. But such is the consequence of a policy wedded to the idea of engineering a negotiated settlement in Rhodesia, since only with such guarantees will the minority government be amenable to discussing a transition to majority rule. Unfortunately for the success of current U.S. policy, the guarantee of social and economic security for the whites is highly unpalatable to the African nationalists. A negotiated "compromise" which provides majority rule but without the power to restructure Rhodesian economic and social life so as to redirect the country's resources toward the African population is hardly likely to be attractive to any African group that perceives a chance of gaining power outside the framework of such negotiations. Thus African politicians who lack the independent source of power that military resources provide have been willing to compromise on the issue of "minority rights," while the Patriotic Front, which possesses such resources, has not. This is the central reality of the Rhodesian crises. Since the goals of the Patriotic Front and the government of Ian Smith are inherently irreconcilable, once both sides could claim significant military capability the potential for a genuine compromise between them became exceedingly marginal.

Henry Kissinger understood this. His strategy for engineering a "moderate solution" was therefore not based upon the willingness of the Patriotic Front and Ian Smith to compromise, but rather on the willingness and ability of third parties to the dispute to force compromise upon them. Each of the combatants in the dispute was, and is, vitally dependent on outside support—the Smith government on South Africa for military supplies, oil, and an outlet to the sea, and the Patriotic Front on Mozambique, Tanzania, Angola, and Zambia for access to military assistance and sanctuary. Since all of these "third parties" have important reasons for desiring an end to the turmoil in Rhodesia, the possibility existed that they would force the Rhodesian/Zimbabwean combatants to accept a compromise solution—i.e., some form of majority rule with strong guarantees of security for the whites. This was the linchpin of the strategy devised by Kissinger and followed by the Carter administration, and it failed to work. Neither South Africa nor the frontline African states have been willing or able to exert the requisite pressure on their respective "clients" to bring about a negotiated settlement. Instead the guerrilla struggle has intensified and the possibility of direct Soviet/Cuban involvement has continued and, if anything, grown.

Despite its lack of success, the Carter administration has dog-

U.S. CREDIBILITY: RHODESIA/ZIMBABWE

gedly persisted in pushing its notion of a negotiated compromise onto the Rhodesian crisis.* The dangers in doing so may prove to be significant. The administration's task has been seriously complicated by Ian Smith who, in response to South African and other international pressure, has unilaterally orchestrated his own version of the "majority rule with minority rights" theme—the Internal Settlement.† This development has set up reverberations in domestic American politics which may well fundamentally undermine the Carter policy. As far as the politics of sub-Saharan Africa are concerned, the Rhodesian internal settlement has been a total nonstarter. Because it excludes the Patriotic Front—i.e., those African groups with real power resources in the form of military capability—and because of the place it provides for Ian Smith and the white minority in the future of Rhodesia, the internal settlement has been universally rejected by African governments as the basis for a transition to genuine majority rule. At the moment, any outside power that acted so as to bolster it would be cast in the role of supporter of white minority domination in southern Africa. The Carter administration, recognizing this and realizing that for the United States to be in this role would invite the very development that its entire

---

*The shape of the compromise—the Anglo-American plan—has been continually modified in response to the strong objections of the Patriotic Front and their African backers to the extensive guarantees of "minority rights." Of course, this has made the deal much less attractive to the regime in Salisbury.

†Launched in February 1978, the Internal Settlement is an agreement between Ian Smith and three prominent African politicians for a transition to a majority rule form of government. Modeled on the original Kissinger proposal for a Rhodesian settlement, it includes very strong provisions for insuring the security of the white minority. The 260,000 whites will for ten years be guaranteed twenty-eight seats in a Parliament of 100. This will allow them to block any constitutional changes sponsored by representatives of the country's 6.7 million African citizens. Furthermore, there are guarantees for whites against the nationalization of property, against the termination of government pensions (even for those who leave the country), and against "political" interference in the military, judiciary, police, and civil service. The latter would prevent large-scale preferential recruitment of Africans, and thus leave Europeans in control of these vital institutions within the political system.

The main thing that distinguishes the African politicans that have joined Smith in the internal settlement from those that lead the Patriotic Front, and have refused, is that the former lack any independent military capability. Lacking an independent means for coming to power, they have had to accept the alternative, however odious, offered by Smith.

Rhodesian policy is designed to avoid—the direct involvement of the Soviets and Cubans to the applause of the states of Black Africa—has carefully eschewed actions that could be seen as supportive of the internal settlement. Unfortunately for the administration, however, the domestic audience for its foreign policy pronouncements may not interpret events in the same manner as its external audience. To a substantial segment of the U.S. Congress the internal settlement looks very much like just what President Carter and his spokesmen have been calling for since the administration assumed office—a negotiated agreement between African political leaders and the Smith regime which offers a peaceful transition to majority rule with protection for minority rights. Having based its public explanation of Rhodesian policy on the absolute need for the avoidance of violence in the creation of a settlement,* the administration is hard-pressed to defend to its domestic audience the continued actions that undermine the internal settlement, and thus aid the insurgent groups who are seeking to undo it by force of arms. Thus in the early Summer of 1978 the Congress voted to lift American compliance with UN-sponsored sanctions against Rhodesia by the end of the year—a move that would substantially bolster the political, economic, and military strength of the Smith regime's internal settlement, and thus firmly cast the United States in the unfortunate role of a defender of continued white domination in southern Africa. The administration avoided the immediate collapse of its African policy because of certain conditions written into the House and Senate resolutions. The Senate version requires the President to lift sanctions if Ian Smith and his colleagues make a "good faith" effort to negotiate with the Patriotic Front, and if the Salisbury regime holds free elections under international supervision. The House version drops the negotiation condition, simply requiring elections. The inclusion of these requirements, particularly the Senate version, was hailed in the media as a victory for the administration's policies, but unfortunately for the President they constitute little more than a postponement of the collapse of his diplomatic position in Africa. Ian Smith can relatively easily agree to enter into negotiations with Nkomo and Mugabe of the Patriotic Front.

---

*Thus in a typical statement of this view, Ambassador Young told the UN Security Council on March 14, 1978: "Most important of all, we must not resign ourselves that the birth of a new nation must be bloody and violent. We see no reason that we cannot find a peaceful solution to the differences which still exist among the parties." This speech was reprinted and distributed by the Department of State, Bureau of Public Affairs, Office of Public Communications.

He is not required to come to any agreement, and can make the absence of such agreement appear to be a result of his opponent's intransigence. He has done this before.* As far as elections are concerned, these are already scheduled for early December 1978.† In other words, the administration was able to extract from the Congress, and only barely, a postponement of the collapse of its policy for a five-month period, during which time it could continue its two-year-old effort to bring the Patriotic Front, or some significant faction of it, into a settlement with Ian Smith.

In sum, by committing itself to a negotiated solution in Rhodesia—i.e., to "non-violence," compromise, and the protection of minority rights, while at the same time espousing majority rule—the Carter administration has adopted a policy whose effect is more favorable to the white minority, seeking against all odds to retain its "way of life" in southern Africa, than it is to the African nationalists. This has occurred not out of deceit or malevolence but rather because U.S. policymakers, in their search to find a formula that might forestall Soviet involvement, have ignored the historical and structural realities of the Rhodesian crisis. However unfortunate they may be, these realities create a context within which the otherwise laudable values of non-violence, compromise, and minority rights function to inhibit the reversal of a condition of racial domination and privilege. As a consequence, current policy has placed the United States on a trajectory that is likely to bring it once again into a position where it is identified with the cause of the whites in southern Africa.

One scenario whereby this position may be reached has already been developed. Congress, acting on the values and policy framework set out by the Carter administration itself, may force a lifting of economic sanctions, and thereby place the United States behind a settlement that is generally viewed within Africa as a means to maintain white privilege. This, however, is not the only conceivable scenario. It is possible, although not very likely, that a settlement could be reached between the Rhodesian government and the externally based insurgents, or some major faction of them. This would

---

*Most notably at the Geneva Conference fiasco of December 1976.

†The Salisbury regime may have grave difficulty holding countrywide elections. The Patriotic Front has committed itself to disrupt them, and has infiltrated thousands of cadre into Rhodesia for this purpose. If the failure to hold effective elections is attributable to the Patriotic Front, it is unlikely that the Congressmen who voted to lift economic sanctions will consider this failure a reason to continue punishing the Salisbury regime.

be most likely to occur through a dual process whereby increasing economic and military pressure leads the Rhodesian government to drop some of its demands for "security guarantees" and one of the Patriotic Front's two major factions, responding to this alteration in Smith regime demands, splits off to join an expanded internal settlement.* Such a development might be viewed as a success for Carter administration policy. With the Patriotic Front split, the unified stance of the African states against the Smith-engineered settlement would in all probability come to an end. At that point, U.S. support for the compromise would no longer be tantamount to an anti-African stance. More important, problems would immediately be created for the Soviets and Cubans, since direct involvement by them to undermine such a settlement would not automatically be defined as opposition to minority rule. Indeed, the difficulty for the Communist powers would probably be especially acute since the faction backed most enthusiastically by the Soviets, that of Joshua Nkomo, is also the most likely candidate to abandon the Patriotic Front and come to terms with Ian Smith. If these developments can be viewed as a success for U.S. policy, it is a success that is likely to be only short-lived.

If one fundamental obstacle to a peaceful resolution to the Rhodesian "crises" is the existence of a racial minority searching for some substitute for political power as a guarantee of its social and economic privilege, another is the intense factional strife among and within the African political groupings. In Rhodesia, as elsewhere in post-colonial Africa, the struggle to wrest political power from the Europeans will surely be followed by the struggle over how and by whom that power will be exercised. While such a pattern is common in states forged out of anti-colonial movements, the Rhodesian situation can be distinguished by the foundation of distrust and animosity that has been laid during many years of intra-African political factionalism.† The history of Rhodesian African nationalism

---

*The Congressional action on sanctions has reduced the likelihood of such a development by holding out the prospect of a reprieve for the Salisbury government. It can now express a willingness to join the Patriotic Front in a conference, without making any actual commitments, hold the elections scheduled for early December, and fully expect U.S. economic sanctions to be lifted. With economic relations with the United States restored, the economic prospects of the regime would improve, morale would be boosted, and a deteriorating military situation would be ameliorated as access to new arms supplies would be facilitated.

†In Rhodesia the struggle to oust the European minority and the struggle for leadership of the majority African population have essentially been occurring

U.S. CREDIBILITY: RHODESIA/ZIMBABWE

since the late 1950's has been marked by a situation in which ethnic difference, ideological divergence, strategic disagreement, generational membership, and personal ambition have combined to create the bitterest and bloodiest form of internecine conflict. If one combines the absence of trust between leaders, the old scores waiting to be settled, and the ethnic and ideological animosities, with the fact that in a post-insurgency situation many thousands of people will continue to have access to arms, then one has a formula for extensive violence and instability during a lengthy period of political consolidation. This would be true even if a settlement were reached which completely ended the externally based insurgency by including both ZANU and ZAPU wings of the Patriotic Front.* But this being a very unlikely development, armed opposition to any new government from the "rump" of the Patriotic Front can be added to the above equation.

The foundation for instability inherent in the dynamics of the nationalist politics of Rhodesia/Zimbabwe should concern the Carter administration because by adopting the Kissinger strategy of engineering a solution for that country's domestic crises, and by sponsoring a specific formula for it, the administration has placed the United States in the position of guarantor of the settlement that emerges.† Having insinuated itself into the internal strife of Rhodesia, the United States is likely to find itself caught in the internal strife of the Zimbabwe it helped create. Given the complexity, longevity, and inherent intractability, at least over the short run, of the many unresolved conflicts facing that country, both between Europeans and Africans, and among Africans themselves,

simultaneously. There is no indication, however, that the second struggle will be resolved at the same time as the first one.

*The Patriotic Front is an extremely tenuous alliance. Its two major organizational constituents, ZANU and ZAPU, continue their separate existence and control their own military wings. They have been the bitterest of rivals for nearly twenty years, and the intermittent bloody conflict that has marked their relationship reportedly continues to the present. It is highly unlikely that this alliance of political enemies would survive the end of white rule. It should also be noted that the unity and discipline existing within ZANU and ZAPU, and particularly the former, is highly problematic. An end to racial rule could well witness the splintering of these groupings on lines reflecting generational, ideological, personal, and ethnic differences.

†It should be noted that in Kissinger's plan Great Britain was given the "honor" of being the sole sponsor of whatever settlement emerged. It was the Carter administration that brought the United States into partnership with the U.K. in the sponsorship of the "Anglo-American Plan."

that is not a very encouraging prospect. For an American administration concerned about projecting its ability to effectively exercise power in peripheral areas, and faced with a domestic constituency highly suspicious of committing resources for such purposes, it is a highly dangerous one. The situation has the unfortunate hallmark of the now proverbial quagmire. Having sponsored an "emergent" settlement, the United States could well find that the chief requirement for its implementation was the provision of internal security. The new Zimbabwe government, however, would most likely be sorely lacking in capacity within this area. Consequently, in order to meet its "commitments," the United States would now have to provide security, among other forms of aid, to a government whose popular support is questionable and which is the target of numerous well-armed and experienced insurgent groups. Moreover, since any negotiated settlement would contain some protection for the position of Rhodesian whites, the opposition to it can be expected to focus on this aspect of the emergent regime in its propaganda. Consequently, the United States would not be able to avoid the onus of aiding the interests of white settlers in southern Africa.

There is no gainsaying the unpleasant nature of the realities that constitute the current Rhodesia/Zimbabwe situation. Whatever might once have been possible, the legacy of three-quarters of a century of racial rule in that country has now bequeathed a political context in which majority rule will preclude the enjoyment of those rights deemed important by the minority, and in which a lengthy period of violent political conflict lies in the immediate future. However tragic this reality may be, a foreign policy that hopes for success cannot afford to ignore it. This is precisely what U.S. policymakers have done. Motivated by a desire to maintain an image of U.S. credibility, they have placed the prestige of the United States behind an effort to produce a settlement which in the abstract seems laudable enough (a compromise producing multiracial harmony, peace, prosperity, and security for all Rhodesians) but which, ignoring the hard realities which created the crises in the first place, must be considered utopian. As such the actual effect of their policy is likely to be the reverse of what was intended. Having placed U.S. power behind goals which are precluded by the structure of the situation, the end result of current policy will be a demonstration of the limits of that power. Rather than enhancing, the policy will ultimately contribute to undermining the credibility of the United States as a global power.

Zaire. The difficulties faced by the Carter administration in demonstrating U.S. credibility in the Angolan, Ethiopian, and Rhodesian situations may help explain its reaction to the rebellion in Zaire's Shaba Province in the Spring of 1978. It is not clear whether high administration officials really believed that the Cubans and Soviets were responsible for this threat to the Mobutu regime, whether they simply charged them with this responsibility in order to create a case of Communist "intervention" against which the United States could effectively demonstrate its resolve, or some combination of the two. What *is* clear about this episode is that the policy adopted involved the creation of a series of illusions. The first of these involved the technical question of direct Cuban/Soviet involvement in the Shaba rebellion. At best a gross exaggeration reminiscent of the anti-Communist hysteria at the height of the Cold War, and at worst a sheer fabrication, the charge to this effect made by the President himself now appears to have been based on a combination of half-truths and of shreds of circumstantial evidence relayed from unreliable sources. Careful scrutiny of the evidence for the charge failed to convince even those in the American government who approached the matter with some degree of skepticism, and the Carter administration itself moved rapidly away from its original position. Thus a month after the President had repeatedly charged Cuban "responsibility" for the Shaba fighting, Secretary of State Vance was telling Congress that Cuban involvement had been "blown out of proportion . . . in the papers and the media."[56] What the Secretary neglected to mention was that it was the administration itself that had fed the press the information that resulted in the illusion of Communist intervention in Shaba. Indeed despite administration back-pedaling on the issue, the Shaba "crisis" has become fixed in the media, the public mind, and the language of international affairs as an instance of Communist intervention.

The second illusion introduced by the administration's Zaire policy is related to the first, but more profound in its implications. It involves the utilization of an external explanation for a problem that is in fact produced by internal causes. The evidence of economic and political disintegration in contemporary Zaire is widely known and acknowledged; its manifestations are legion.[57] Zaire's potential riches and the national opportunities they present have been squandered through its government's ill-conceived economic policies, the extraordinary venality of the political elite, and a system of ubiquitous public corruption on the most grandiose scale. As the usable road network is gradually surrendered back to the bush for lack of maintenance, as agriculture declines precipitously as a result of neglect, and as government-sponsored health and educational facilities collapse, the national economic disaster reflected in statistics on GNP, trade, and foreign indebtedness impacts upon the average citizen. Official Zaire government statistics reveal that the real income of the ordinary worker in Kinshasa has declined by as much as 75 percent since independence.* Those living in interior towns and the rural areas have suffered an even greater decline. Some sense of the economic degradation that the ordinary citizen has experienced under the Mobutu regime can be gleaned from the following comparisons: In 1960 it took five days to earn enough to pay for a sack of manioc, a staple food; today it takes seventeen days; one kilogram of river fish could be purchased in 1960 with the wages of a single day's labor; today the same amount of fish would require ten days' work.[58] The political ramifications of this economic decline have been the predictable ones. Knowledgeable observers agree that popular support for the Mobutu regime is nil. During 1977 armed rebellions broke out in Bandundu and Kasai regions, in addition to Shaba. There is little doubt that these have a popular basis, with those not actively supporting the rebels indifferent to the fate of the Mobutu regime. After the Shaba rebellion of 1978 even the ultraconservative and anti-Communist journal *To the Point* reported that the population is "being driven into the arms of the rebels, by poverty, hunger, disappointment and chaos as much as by the brutality, terror and corruption of the Zairean army in their midst."[59] The Zairean General Dikuta, who led the government's forces against the rebels in Shaba, is reported to have made the astonishing admission that "next time the natives from the border areas will stand 100 percent behind the rebels."[60]

In spite of the incontrovertible evidence of internal collapse, the Carter administration chose to blame outside intervention for the threat to the Mobutu regime. This failure to accept the indigenous basis of threats to a U.S. client is the second illusion built into the Carter policy on Zaire. It fits into the conventional American policy paradigm which for decades has provided the same simple explanation for all losses in U.S. influence abroad—they are produced by the machinations of Communist foreign policy. The "myth of the outside agitator" created the foundation for two further

---

*The Index of Purchasing Power dropped from 100 in 1960 to 64 in 1971, and then to 26 by March 1976. The source for these statistics is the official national labor organization in Zaire—Union Nationale des Travailleurs Zairois. They are presented in Rymenam, "The Zairian Fiction" (see note 57).

illusions—the mobilization of a pan-African collective security force to protect Mobutu from rebellions that his corrupt and unreliable army is not capable of handling, and the belief that through increased assistance long-term stability can be obtained. The pan-African force would repel outside intervention, while Western aid nursed the Mobutu regime back to a position in which it could do so by itself. Unfortunately for the success of this policy, the context in which President Carter announced U.S. support for the idea of an African military force to provide security for Mobutu was hardly conducive to lending validity and legitimacy to the idea. First, the fact that French and Belgian paratroopers had already landed in Shaba with U.S. assistance, and that the idea for an African force was sponsored by the French Premier, and announced by the American President, took a good deal of respectability away from the concept. Second, the reality that only a few sub-Saharan African countries actually came forward to back the idea, that they were willing to contribute only a few troops, and that as a group they constituted the most clear examples of French "client-states" undercut the claim that what was being touted was actually an *African* means to prevent outside intervention. As such the idea appears to have come to little. Finally, the greatest illusion of all may be that by protecting Mobutu from his internal opposition and by the application of increased amounts of technical and financial assistance the West can reimpose stability on the Zaire regime. Again, the evidence that Zaire's problems are systemic, that the Mobutu regime is a part of the problem, and that in a real sense the regime has already crumbled from within is not really open to question. The latest Belgian and French intervention has not defeated the Shaba rebels any more than the Moroccan-French involvement a year earlier did. Most informed observers have little doubt that there will be a third installment to the Shaba rebellion and that similar uprisings elsewhere in the huge country can be expected also.

Because it is unresponsive to the substance of the problems affecting Zaire, the policy followed by the Carter administration in response to the events in Shaba contains serious potential costs. The diplomatic interest of the United States in being considered a friendly outside power by the states of sub-Saharan Africa was hurt by this policy. Most states in the region, seeing through the illusion of Soviet/Cuban intervention, refused to back the concept of a "Pan-African" force. Julius Nyerere, perhaps the most politically influential leader in the area, especially among the younger generation of intellectuals and politicians, and General Olusegun Obasanjo of Nigeria, the head of the most economically powerful and politically influential state in the region, both made major public declarations defining the Shaba situation as an internal affair in which Western powers had intervened to protect foreign economic interests, and attacking the concept of a French organized "Pan-African" security force as an instrument of neo-colonialism. Addressing the assembled heads of state at the annual Organization of African Unity meeting, General Obasanjo declared: "We totally reject as an instrument of neo-colonialism any collective security scheme for Africa fashioned and teleguided from outside Africa for economic, political or military interest of any superpower bloc."[61] The unfortunate aspect to the support provided by the United States for intervention in Zaire is not simply that the legitimating "Pan-African" force failed to materialize, but that the Carter administration placed the United States behind the ex-colonial power, Belgium, and the most active neo-colonial power, France, in their efforts to protect and extend their political and economic interests. Given the sensitivity in Africa to the colonial past and to the dangers of European neo-colonialism, this can hardly be viewed as in the long-term diplomatic interests of the United States.* To be sure, the intervention and the idea of a covering Pan-African force had its supporters among African heads of state. Léopold Senghor, Félix Houphouet-Boigny, Omar Bongo, and Emperor Bokassa constitute the major African backers of the idea. Unfortunately, it is difficult to draw encouragement about the United States' future diplomatic position in Africa from the composition of this small group—two septuagenarians, a man who owes his position to the military intervention of the French, and a petty tyrant with delusions of grandeur.

U.S. support for the type of intervention that occurred in Shaba may well have economic as well as diplomatic costs, especially if it represents part of a pattern to be repeated in the future. Earlier in this essay it was argued that the structural realities of African eco-

---

*Thus Julius Nyerere, in the statement mentioned above, told a specially called assemblage of foreign diplomats in the Tanzanian capital that "This talk in Europe about a Pan-African Security Force *is an insult to Africa.* . . . It makes little difference if the European initiators of this plan find Africans to do their fighting for them. There were Africans who fought with the colonial invaders. . . . We must reject the principle that external powers have the right to maintain in power African governments which are universally recognized to be corrupt, or incompetent, or a bunch of murderers, when their people try to make a change" (emphasis added). Excerpts of Nyerere's speech are reprinted in *International Bulletin* 5, 13 (July 3, 1978), p. 5.

nomic systems were such that radical political change would not threaten the continuation of extensive economic relations with the West. This conclusion was based upon the assumption that those individuals or groups holding political power were oriented toward economic advance. The discussion of the actual policies followed by radical governments in Africa confirmed the existence of such political elites. There are indications from the second Shaba rebellion that the rebel leaders were similarly oriented—for example, the plan for the rebellion, called "Operation Dove," apparently included setting up a provincial revolutionary government in Kolwezi with three Belgians and one Frenchman participating, and damage and sabotage to the mining installations in the town of Kolwezi was largely avoided.* There are, however, also indications of the emergence of a very different kind of political orientation within the Shaba rebellion. Reports from refugees indicated that shortly after occupying Kolwezi the discipline of the rebel force broke down with European civilians becoming the object of wanton killing. The same reports indicate that Frenchmen (and those mistaken for being French), as well as those who looked like Moroccans, were the special targets for these attacks, and that unemployed youth of Kolwezi town joined the rebel soldiers in the killing.[62] Since it was the French and Moroccans that suppressed the uprising a year earlier, the massacre of whites that occurred in 1978 can be viewed as the outpouring of spontaneous vengeance for the earlier intervention and for the brutal repression of the Shaba population at the hands of Mobutu's army that followed it. What we may have been witnessing in Kolwezi is the emergence of a sort of populist antiforeign hatred, born out of the frustration created by utter impotence in the face of European power. This could be the wellspring of a contemporary "Luddite" movement in which all manifestations of the foreign presence become targets for destruction, regardless of the long-term economic consequences. Indeed, if the economic interests of Europeans lead them to maintain Mobutu, and if under

---

*See *Africa Confidential* 19, 12 (June 9, 1978), pp. 4 and 8, and the on-the-spot report from Kolwezi by Erich Wiedemann, editor of *Der Spiegel*: "The highly sensitive copper and cobalt electrolysis installations at Kamoto are undamaged. Only the mineshafts in Kipushi and Musonoi are filled with water because the pumps malfunctioned. The hundred-ton trucks in the open pit mine at Kamoto are parked in rows, as if waiting to be loaded. It is obvious that at the outset the attackers wanted to destroy nothing. That only came later. They even assured Belgian technicians that they and their families would not be harmed if they kept the mines running" ("My Brother Does Not Have a Head Anymore," *Der Spiegel* 32, 22 [May 19, 1978], pp. 128-33).

his regime the local population derives little benefit from the existence of these interests, then there is a certain short-term logic in eliminating the European interests so as to remove the *raison d'etat* for intervention. The conclusion that follows from this analysis is that intervention by the Western powers in Zaire could spark a movement which would profoundly threaten the very economic interests they acted to protect—continued access to supplies of copper and cobalt and security for sunk investments in the mining industry.

Finally, what of the effect of the Zaire policy on U.S. credibility, its image of determination and effectiveness in the projection of its power abroad? As far as the short run is concerned, a case can be made for certain gains on this dimension. The FNLC (Front National de Liberation du Congo) was prevented from taking Shaba province and toppling Mobutu, and a message of a sort was sent to the Soviets and Cubans about the U.S. will and ability to defend its definition of the national interest. One can question whether these "gains" outweigh the diplomatic and potential long-term economic costs of the policy. One can also question whether a demonstration of credibility was in fact necessary. The secret communication sent by Fidel Castro to President Carter, warning of an impending Shaba rebellion led by exiles in Angola and describing his efforts to prevent the action, indicates that Cuban sensitivity to U.S. perceptions and reactions already existed. The more important question, however, about the credibility gains deriving from the Zaire policy concern the relation between the short and long term. Can the policy being followed in fact put the Zaire economy back together again, and resurrect political support for Mobutu, or does the second Shaba military intervention simply involve a temporary stopgap measure, as did the first? All odds would seem to be on the latter. Why should the provision of training and equipment by the Western powers now turn the Zaire army into a dependable fighting force when such assistance over a ten-year period failed utterly to do so? Similarly with the civil administration. For years representatives of the IMF and the World Bank, officials of the U.S. Embassy in Kinshasa, and advisors from France and Belgium have assisted the Zaire government with planning and administration. Can the placement of a few more IMF officials at the top of Zaire's Central Bank and Finance Ministry and in key departments and parastatal organizations, as has just occurred, be expected to bring efficiency and effectiveness to a public service riddled with corruption, mismanagement, and disinterest?* And even if these inter-

---

*The National Bank of Zaire reports that in 1971 fully *60 percent* of current government revenue was lost or used for purposes other than official ones. See **Banque Nationale du Zaire,** *Rapport Annuel 1974,* p. 121.

national civil servants manage to bring a degree of probity into the operation of Zaire's financial institutions, the direct beneficiaries will be international creditors—not Zaire's population, upon whose support the Mobutu regime will ultimately stand or fall. The political failure of the regime would seem to be so total as to be irreparable. It can be measured by the precipitous decline, relative to the colonial period, in agricultural production, transport and communications infrastructure, educational and health services, real wages, and subsistence levels—i.e., in the standard of living of the vast majority of the population—and also by the fact that in order to survive the regime has been forced to turn to foreigners, including the ex-colonial power, to run the governmental machinery, control the economy, and supply internal security.*

One final point remains. The abject dependence of the Mobutu regime on Western governments and the relinquishing of institutional control to their representatives not only adds to the political disaffection within Zaire, but may well result in Zaire becoming a pariah within regional politics. This policy of turning much of the government over to foreigners, a policy supported by the United States as a means to shore up the Mobutu regime, may come to be viewed within sub-Saharan Africa as a reversion to colonialism.† As such, the Mobutu regime could become a glaring symbol of the

---

*The dependence on Belgian, French, and Moroccan troops as a substitute for the Zaire armed forces is only the most glaring manifestation of the absence of genuine sovereignty. As the price for the rescue of the Zaire economy, Mobutu has had to accept the appointment of Western specialists to key positions in his government and to adopt as his own an economic plan drafted by a committee of outside powers. Thus the "Mobutu Plan" to rescue the economy over the next two years was actually devised by top officials from the United States, France, Belgium, Britain, and West Germany, at a meeting in Paris on June 6, and ratified a week later in Brussels by additional representatives from Italy, Holland, Canada, Japan, Iran, the IMF, the World Bank, the Common Market Commission, and Zaire. In exchange for one billion dollars in aid over the next two years, Mobutu had to agree to place Western representatives at the top of key Zaire government institutions. Thus IMF representatives will oversee the Finance Ministry and the National Bank, and other outside specialists will be distributed throughout the governmental apparatus—in transport, communications, defense, and the nationalized mining industry. The terms of the economic bail-out led one State Department official to remark that Mobutu was being made "a ward of the court" (*International Bulletin* 5, 12 [June 19, 1978], p. 1).

†Note the statement by Julius Nyerere quoted in the footnote on p. 54. Other African countries, as well as Zaire prior to the current crises, have been heavily dependent on foreign advisors and assistants. What distinguishes the contemporary Zaire situation is the dramatic and *public* manifestation of the utter abjectness of this dependence.

failure of African independence and a testament to African inferiority. Close association with such a regime would thus carry a stigma that would not be particularly helpful to the diplomatic position of the United States in the region.*

In short, looking beyond the suppression of the latest Shaba rebellion the Zaire situation does not present an encouraging environment for demonstrations of the effectiveness of U.S. power. On the contrary, the intractability of the Mobutu regime's problems and its utter political and economic bankruptcy would appear to create an ideal scenario for casting the United States in the role that President Nixon once referred to as "the helpless and pitiful giant." Thus in the medium term, the policy adopted in response to the Shaba rebellion may well detract from the credibility of U.S. power. In addition the policy contains the seeds of ancillary costs to U.S. diplomatic and economic interests.

---

*In support of Carter policy, one could point to the Soviet/Cuban involvement in Angola, noting the crucial role that the Communist states have played in maintaining the MPLA regime, and ask why Western support for Mobutu should carry a stigma if similar support by the Communists for Neto is considered legitimate aid? The question, however, reveals a lack of appreciation for the historical context within which perceptions are formed. Two things distinguish the Zaire and Angolan situations that are crucial in this respect. First, the fact that colonialism in Africa was a West European phenomenon means that any new intervention with which these erstwhile metropoles are associated carries with it a special opprobrium from which those states not associated with the history of colonialism are immune. Second, and more important, is the period in the post-colonial experience during which the outside involvement has occurred. In Angola the Cubans and Soviets are viewed as aiding in the birth of a new nation—providing the resources that the irresponsible Portuguese parent neglected to provide. In contrast, Zaire has been an independent state for over fifteen years. The reintroduction of European control, therefore, appears as a return to the colonialism that had previously ended.

IV

CONCLUSION

In June 1976, upon his return from the first visit of an American Secretary of State to sub-Saharan Africa, Henry Kissinger declared before the House Committee on International Relations that along with preventing foreign intervention, and promoting cooperation among the communities in southern Africa, *the goal of U.S. policy was "to prevent the radicalization of Africa."*[63] Upon his election, President Carter disclaimed such a characteristically "cold war" posture toward African developments. In short order, however, events in the Horn, in Rhodesia, and in Zaire, with which the Soviet Union and Cuba were either involved, potentially involved, or allegedly involved, shifted the policy emphasis of his administration in precisely the direction he had disavowed. The "danger" of radicalization and concomitant Soviet involvement have come to dominate U.S. policy concerns regarding sub-Saharan Africa, and the fashioning of an appropriate response to this "danger" has moved to the upper reaches of the foreign policy agenda. This paper has been concerned with whether the "dangers" that have occupied so much of the administration's time and have figured so centrally in the statements of its spokesmen are in fact real, and, in that light, whether the policy designed as a response is appropriate to the national interest of the United States.

Radical political transformation in sub-Saharan Africa, especially when it occurs with substantial assistance from the Soviet Union, is usually viewed as dangerous to the United States in one or both of two ways—as a threat to certain tangible military and/or economic interests, and as a challenge to the credibility of U.S. power in the area, which if not met would weaken the position of the United States within the global system. Careful analysis of the context within which such radical transformations have occurred, or are occurring, reveals, however, that the calculation of these threats is based on assumptions that are no longer rooted in the facts of the real world. As such the "threats" are more myth than reality, and the policies developed to respond to them are dangerously "out of sync" with the environment in which they must operate. Significant strategic interests of the United States, or the West generally, in Africa south of the Sahara simply do not exist—the scenario of a blockade of Western shipping lanes being not only far-fetched but logically implausible. In contrast, very significant U.S. economic interests are found in the region. These, however, are not threatened by radical political transformation. Both the structure of the economic systems of African states and changes in the international economic system have led to a situation in which radical states are no less desirous than so-called moderate states of maintaining active trading relations with the West, and obtaining access to Western capital markets, managerial know-how, and technology. The "credibility threat" is a more complicated affair because the behavior of U.S. statesmen, as well as the actions of the Soviet Union, are involved in its creation. Maintenance of U.S. credibility involves a concern with the psychological dimension of power—with how a set of events is perceived. A given Soviet move becomes a threat to U.S. "credibility" only when it is perceived by various audiences (the Soviets themselves, U.S. allies, the American public, etc.) as constituting a significant challenge to American interests, influence, desires, etc. When U.S. government spokesmen define Soviet moves in this manner, even when no tangible interests are at stake, they contribute to such a perception. If the United States could "propose and dispose" worldwide—i.e., if it could exercise effective global hegemony—then the definition of every Soviet action outside its circumscribed sphere as a challenge to U.S. credibility would pose little problem. Under such circumstances successful demonstrations of U.S. "resolve" would be guaranteed, and frequent opportunities to display America's will to act would indeed provide a means to underscore the credibility of U.S. power. Serious problems arise, however, when hegemony is *not* assured: when situations arise that preclude a successful exercise of power, or where the costs of success are prohibitive. In such situations the definition of a threat to the United States, irrespective of whether or not tangible interests are at stake, creates the basis for undermining credibility rather than enhancing it. Thus if the Soviet Union is involved in situations where an effective exercise of U.S. power at feasible cost is highly problematic and in which no tangible U.S. interests are at issue, a concern for the credibility of U.S. power would dictate that government spokesmen avoid defining the situation as a direct challenge to the United States. This is the lesson that the current situation in sub-Saharan Africa teaches, and that the Carter administration has failed to learn.

I am not suggesting that under contemporary circumstances

CONCLUSION

the United States adopt a weak or isolationist foreign policy—i.e., an unwillingness, on principle, to exercise power abroad. Rather what I believe these circumstances make imperative are two things: first, a rejoining of the concern for the credibility of U.S. power with a concern for the protection of tangible interests; and second, a sensitivity to the political reverberations created by the use of that power among states other than the Soviet Union. Instead of being an autonomous and overriding criterion in action decisions, credibility ought to be established and maintained as a concomitant of the willingness to use American power in defense of demonstrably established tangible interests. The criterion for engaging in a test of credibility, and for deciding on the extent of resources to be committed to it, would be the significance of the U.S. stake—diplomatic, strategic, or economic—in any given situation. The use of power would be scaled to the nature of the national interest involved, up to and including military intervention. Intervention, however, would be directed to obtaining some tangible goal, with the intangible psychological aspect of power—credibility—following as a "side-benefit." In a world in which power is diffused, the pursuit of tangible interests can set up political reverberations among numerous states. Thus, policy must be sensitive to the historical and political context of any given situation so as to avoid acts which have unintended and unforeseen negative ramifications, placing in jeopardy other interests, or even the long-term security of the very interest being pursued in the short term.

In regard specifically to sub-Saharan Africa, the foregoing analysis implies a number of guidelines for future policy. The nature of America's tangible economic and diplomatic interests in the area suggests a policy of limited goals—access for U.S. firms to trade, invest, and operate on terms no less favorable than those offered to the businesses of other countries; a relatively secure supply of certain critical minerals; and support for or at least the avoidance of hostility toward U.S. positions in international forums and multilateral negotiations. The structurally conditioned need of the African economies for external sources of capital, technology, and managerial know-how suggests the most appropriate means for U.S. policy to foster these objectives. The ability of the U.S. government to facilitate or hinder the flow of capital, technology, and management abroad, its resources in the area of financial and technical assistance, and its influence in such multilateral bodies as the World Bank and the IMF provide a natural quid pro quo for policies of African states that are favorable to the United States. In the application of this policy based on reciprocity, the ideological coloration of a particular regime should be considered irrelevant—it is the actual behavior of the regime in regard to the above limited objectives that counts. Because the interests in question are for the most part not vital, and because even when they are, as in the case of critical minerals, political change does not necessarily pose a substantial threat to them, there is no need to impose an American vision of an appropriate "order" in the region, or, to cultivate particularly powerful clients in the area—so-called regional hegemons—to do so in proxy fashion. Such a policy is not only unnecessary but can also be dangerous. Given the limited social base of most African regimes and the resultant transitory nature of their power, if not actual survival, efforts to cultivate "special" relationships may be very costly in the short term, and have considerable unintended costs that are difficult to jettison in the longer run. When one witnesses the apparent desire of the Carter administration to create a "special" relationship with Nigeria because it is allegedly emerging as the major economic and political power in the area—a regional hegemon—one is reminded that in the early 1970's Zaire and its President Mobutu were viewed in Washington in exactly the same manner.

In one particular area—that of southern Africa—a more activist role by the United States than the one suggested above is called for. The stance taken by the United States in regard to the continuation of regimes of white domination in Rhodesia and South Africa will certainly affect the ability of the United States to obtain the diplomatic cooperation of the states of Black Africa. It may also enter into the calculation of African governments in decisions regarding economic relations, particularly as regards access by U.S. companies for purposes of investment, trade, and technology arrangements. Although moving away from current efforts to impose a "peaceful" solution which preserves a political role for the whites would be a step in the right direction, it would not be sufficient to satisfy African expectations. In a situation in which past, and to some extent current, economic and political links have bolstered the white regimes, a posture of complete disinterest and "neutrality" regarding racial rule in Rhodesia and South Africa will not be seen as acceptable. In other words, there is an expectation in the region that the United States should take an active role in eliminating racial rule in southern Africa. Failure to effectively respond to these expectations will entail diplomatic and possibly economic costs. Unfortunately, fashioning a policy to meet these

CONCLUSION

expectations, and so to further American interests in Africa, is made difficult by a variety of political constraints. Thus the policy that would be most satisfying in light of African regional politics would be the provision of military equipment and training to the "liberation movements" operating against Rhodesia and South Africa and the breaking off of all economic relations with the two countries. Neither policy, however, can be feasibly pursued. The option of providing military aid to groups perceived as radical and revolutionary is not something that either the American public or Congress can be expected to accept. The policy of total economic sanctions—an end to trade, investment, technology, and managerial agreements, and the like—would not only probably be impossible to effectively implement, but very strong domestic interest groups would oppose it; economic damage would likely be done to our allies, particularly Great Britain; and, given the U.S. economy's need for certain minerals of South Africa origin, a vital national economic interest would be sacrificed. In light of these constraints, two lines of policy ought to be followed: (1) The United States should provide substantial "humanitarian" aid—food, clothing, medical supplies, funds for educational uses, etc.—to the "liberation" movements. Since there is a lack of unity among those seeking to remove racial rule from Rhodesia and South Africa, and since the United States ought to avoid getting drawn into the conflicts between the various groups, such aid should be channeled through multilateral arrangements. Two such arrangements already exist in the Liberation Committee of the Organization of African Unity and the informal grouping of Presidents of the so-called Front Line states (Tanzania, Zambia, Angola, Mozambique, and Botswana), and these could serve the purpose of allocating U.S. aid. (2) Economic pressure should be applied in a differentiated manner against the South African regime. Investment and technology transfer in areas unrelated to the development and export of critical mineral resources ought to be discouraged by those agencies of the U.S. government that play a role in encouraging, facilitating, and protecting private foreign investment by American corporations and banks. Furthermore, trade in goods other than critical materials ought to be discouraged, and alternative sources for even critical minerals ought to be utilized as far as is possible.

In providing a critique of recent U.S. policy toward sub-Saharan Africa, my main concern has not been to offer a set of alternative policies, but rather to question the appropriateness of the conventional foreign policy paradigm and the set of underlying assumptions about the nature of the international order and America's place in it in terms of which Africa policy has been generated. There is little doubt that elements within the Carter administration are aware that assumptions upon which policy during the 1950's and 1960's was based do not serve adequately in the contemporary world. This group—usually referred to in the media as the "africanists"—has pushed for policies that closely resemble some of the guidelines suggested above, and, from time to time, has succeeded in defining the policy posture of the administration. It has, however, lacked a fully elaborated and articulated foreign policy paradigm which could replace that which served since the end of World War II. That has been its weakness. Whenever some new action by the Russians or Cubans in Africa has raised the salience of the Cold War paradigm, the "africanists" have lost their hold over the direction of administration policy, and a set of policies with a very different thrust, but more consistent with the assumptions and logic of that paradigm, has become dominant. Indeed, the conventional paradigm offers a number of distinct advantages. Its simple dichotomous vision of the world provides an unambiguous guide to action—thus it is attractive to the hard-pressed maker of policy. It is rooted in the political culture of the country at large, and represents an important element in the belief system of powerful constituencies in Congress and the federal bureaucracy—thus it is attractive to the politician. It is associated, at least until the Vietnam debacle, with decades of what in the American viewpoint is an impressive record of foreign policy success—thus it is difficult to jettison for an untried perspective. These advantages, however, relate to domestic politics, not to the substantive relation between the paradigm and the reality it supposedly reflects. The general point of the analysis provided in this paper is that this relation is seriously askew and that therefore policy has been dangerously miscast.

What is called for is the elaboration and articulation of a new perspective that *explicitly* recognizes the changed nature of contemporary circumstances and the U.S. role in them. This means an acceptance of the Soviet Union as a genuine global power *along with the United States*, and a concomitant willingness to accommodate Soviet actions that do not threaten tangible U.S. interests. In other words, it means the adoption of a non-zero-sum view of the relationship between U.S. and Soviet interest and influence, and a reluctance to claim a vital involvement in, and responsibility for, developments throughout the world. Further, it means accepting a genuinely pluralistic world, in which the political identities and

CONCLUSION

economic relationships of states cross-cut the old definition of a world built on two competing "blocs."[64] The working-out of the historical process in Africa reveals that this type of world is indeed emerging. What remains is to see if the United States continues the futile and ultimately dangerous effort to reshape this world in the mold of an outmoded global vision, or if it can respond to changing circumstances with a policy characterized by what Stanley Hoffmann has termed "the imperative of modesty and devolution."[65]

NOTES

1. U.S. Congress, Senate, Committee on Foreign Relations, Subcommittee on African Affairs, *U.S. Policy Toward Africa*, Hearings, March 5, 1976, p. 193.
2. *Ibid.*, *Ambassador Young's African Trip*, Hearings, June 6, 1977, p. 14.
3. David Rees, "Soviet Penetration in Africa," *Conflict Studies* 77 (November 1976): 1. See also Patrick Wall, ed., *The Southern Oceans and the Security of the Free World* (London, 1977), passim.
4. Rees, p. 1.
5. See David Ottaway, "China Gain Is Reported in Mozambique," *Washington Post*, December 3, 1975.
6. *Pravda*, October 8, 1976; reprinted in the *Current Digest of Soviet Press*, V.XXVIII, N. 41, p. 9.
7. Ottaway, *Washington Post*, February 16, 1977.
8. Tom J. Farer, *War Clouds on the Horn of Africa: A Crisis for Detente* (Carnegie Endowment for International Peace, 1976), pp. 104-24.
9. Farer, p. 114.
10. See William J. Foltz, "United States Policy Toward Southern Africa: Economic and Strategic Constraints," *Political Science Quarterly* 92, 1 (Spring 1977): 58.
11. Farer, p. 115.
12. In a recent publication, Michael McGwire, a retired Royal Navy commander and professor of military studies at Dalhousie University, states that "in all essentials the Soviet Navy's strategic mission remains the traditional one of defending the homeland" (*Soviet Naval Developments: Context and Capability* [New York, 1973], p. 518). See also Barry M. Blechman, *The Changing Soviet Navy* (Washington, D.C., 1973), p. 36, and Michael T. Klare, "Superpower Rivalry at Sea," *Foreign Policy* 21 (Winter 1975-76), passim.
13. Farer, p. 114.
14. See U.S. Congress, Senate, Committee on Foreign Relations, *U.S. Corporate Interests in South Africa*, Report, January 1978, p. 7.
15. Foltz, p. 50.
16. See U.S. Bureau of Mines, *Mineral Industries of Africa*, 1976, and U.S. Department of the Interior, *Mining and Minerals Policy*, 1977: "Annual Report of the Secretary of the Interior," p. 152.
17. See U.S. Department of the Interior, p. 24.
18. See *ibid.*, p. 152, and U.S. Bureau of Mines, *Commodity Data Summaries*, 1977.
19. The other major source of platinum group metals is the Soviet Union, from which 30 percent of U.S. imports derive. See U.S. Bureau of Mines, *Mineral Industries of Africa*, 1976, and *Commodity Data Summaries*, 1977, and U.S. Department of the Interior, *Mining and Minerals Policy*, 1977.

NOTES

20. See Karen A. Mingst, "Southern Africa's Commodity Trade with the United States: The Political Impact of Change," *Africa Today* 24, 2 (April-June 1977): 13-14.
21. *Encyclopaedia Britannica*, Micropaedia III, p. S20.
22. U.S. Bureau of Mines, *Commodity Data Summaries*, 1977. The USSR and Zaire are the world's other major producers.
23. See Tami Hultman and Reed Kramer, "South Africa's Rising Nuclear Prowess," *Los Angeles Times*, August 28, 1977.
24. U.S. Department of State, *The Trade Debate*, 1978.
25. U.S. Bureau of Mines, *Mining & Minerals Policy*, 1977, p. 152.
26. U.S. Department of the Interior, p. 152.
27. See *U.S. News and World Report*, December 5, 1977.
28. See U.S. Department of the Interior.
29. See Barclay Bank Group, *Country Reports*, 4 December 1974; Colin Legum, ed., *Africa Contemporary Record*, 1974/1975 (London, 1976), p. B612.
30. See Barclay Bank Group, *Country Reports*, 30 June 1975, 17 May 1976, and 14 December 1977. See also David B. Ottaway, "Drop in Oil Sales Sobers Free-Spending Nigerians," *Washington Post*, April 17, 1978.
31. See Colin Legum, ed., *Africa Contemporary Record*, 1975/76 (London, 1977), p. B477.
32. See *ibid.*, 1970/71 (London, 1972), p. B305.
33. See *ibid.*, 1975/76, p. B707.
34. See "Guinea: Francophone Reconciliation," *Africa Confidential*, 19, 8 (April 14, 1978), p. 6.
35. See Financial Times Ltd., *Mining International Yearbook, 1977* (London, 1977), pp. 179 and 432.
36. *Ibid.*
37. *Ibid.*, p. 488.
38. Legum, ed., *Africa Contemporary Record*, 1975/76, p. B707.
39. *Ibid.*
40. *Ibid.*, 1976/77, p. B458. Texaco and Total, two other U.S. companies, have also resumed production in Angola. See also *Africa Research Bulletin, Financial and Economic Series*, May 5-June 14, 1976, p. 3910.
41. *Africa Confidential*, 19, 2 (January 20, 1978), p. 3.
42. Legum, ed., *Africa Contemporary Record*, 1976/77, p. B458, and "Foreign Firms Return to Angola," *African Development* 10, 11 (November 1976): 1113.
43. See *Africa Confidential*, 19, 2 (January 20, 1978), p. 3.
44. *Washington Post*, February 21, 1977.
45. See "Mozambique: Economic Pragmatism," *Africa Confidential*, 19, 8 (April 14, 1978), pp. 2-4.

NOTES

46. *Ibid.*, p. 3.
47. See *ibid.*, and David Ottaway, *Washington Post*, and *Africa Contemporary Record*, 1976/77, p. B305.
48. See Sir Ronald Prain, "African Mining in the Doldrums," *African Business*, pre-publication issue—June 1978, pp. 14-15.
49. U.S. Congress, Senate, Committee on Foreign Relations, Subcommittee on African Affairs, *Angola*, Hearings, January 29, 1976, p. 8. (Emphasis added.)
50. Jonathan Schell, *The Time of Illusion* (New York, 1976), esp. Part VI.
51. Henry Kissinger, *Nuclear Weapons and Foreign Policy*; quoted in Schell, p. 345.
52. Maxwell Taylor, *The Uncertain Trumpet*; quoted in Schell, pp. 352-53.
53. Taylor; quoted in Schell, p. 353.
54. *New York Times*, July 20, 1978.
55. *Ibid.*
56. *International Bulletin*, July 3, 1978, p. 5.
57. For an excellent and brief summary of the Mobutu regime's record, see Jean Rymenam, "The Zairian Fiction," *Le Monde Diplomatique*, May 1977, pp. 8-11.
58. Calculations were made by Rymenam in *ibid*.
59. "Mbumba's Second Shaba Attack Threat 'No Bluff'," *To the Point* 5, 27 (July 7, 1978), p. 24.
60. *Ibid.*
61. *New York Times*, July 20, 1978.
62. See *Africa Confidential* (June 9, 1978), and Erich Wiedemann's report in *Der Spiegel* (May 29, 1978).
63. U.S. Congress, House, Committee on International Relations, *Report of the Secretary of State on His Trip to Europe, Latin America, and Africa*, June 1976.
64. For an elaboration of this position see Kenneth Jowitt, *Images of Detente and the Soviet Political Order* (Berkeley: Institute of International Studies, University of California, 1977) [Policy Papers in International Affairs], passim.
65. Stanley Hoffmann, "Choices," *Foreign Policy* 12 (Fall 1973): 42.

ROBERT M. PRICE is Associate Professor of Political Science and Associate Director of the Institute of International Studies at the University of California, Berkeley. He is the author of *Society and Bureaucracy in Contemporary Ghana*. His current research focuses on the politics of economic nationalism in sub-Saharan Africa.

INSTITUTE OF INTERNATIONAL STUDIES
UNIVERSITY OF CALIFORNIA, BERKELEY

CARL G. ROSBERG,
Director

Monographs published by the Institute include:

RESEARCH SERIES

1. *The Chinese Anarchist Movement*, by Robert A. Scalapino and George T. Yu ($1.00)
3. *Land Tenure and Taxation in Nepal*, Volume I, *The State as Landlord: Raikar Tenure*, by Mahesh C. Regmi. ($8.75; unbound photocopy)
4. *Land Tenure and Taxation in Nepal*, Volume II, *The Land Grant System: Birta Tenure*, by Mahesh C. Regmi. ($2.50)
6. *Local Taxation in Tanganyika*, by Eugene C. Lee. ($1.00)
7. *Birth Rates in Latin America: New Estimates of Historical Trends*, by O. Andrew Collver. ($2.50)
8. *Land Tenure and Taxation in Nepal*, Volume III, *The Jagir, Rakam, and Kipat Tenure Systems*, by Mahesh C. Regmi ($2.50)
9. *Ecology and Economic Development in Tropical Africa*, edited by David Brokensha. ($8.25; unbound photocopy)
12. *Land Tenure and Taxation in Nepal*, Volume IV, *Religious and Charitable Land Endowments: Guthi Tenure*, by Mahesh C. Regmi ($2.75)
13. *The Pink Yo-Yo: Occupational Mobility in Belgrade, ca 1915-1965*, by Eugene A. Hammel. ($2.00)
14. *Community Development in Israel and the Netherlands: A Comparative Analysis*, by Ralph M. Kramer. ($2.50)
*15. *Central American Economic Integration: The Politics of Unequal Benefits*, by Stuart I. Fagan. ($2.00)
16. *The International Imperatives of Technology: Technological Development and the International Political System*, by Eugene B. Skolnikoff. ($2.95)
*17. *Autonomy or Dependence as Regional Integration Outcomes: Central America*, by Philippe C. Schmitter. ($1.75)
18. *Framework for a General Theory of Cognition and Choice*, by R.M. Axelrod. ($1.50)
19. *Entry of New Competitors in Yugoslav Market Socialism*, by S.R. Sacks. ($2.50)
*20. *Political Integration in French-Speaking Africa*, by Abdul A. Jalloh. ($3.50)
21. *The Desert and the Sown: Nomads in the Wider Society*, ed. by Cynthia Nelson. ($3.50)
22. *U.S.-Japanese Competition in International Markets: A Study of the Trade-Investment Cycle in Modern Capitalism*, by John E. Roemer. ($3.95)
23. *Political Disaffection Among British University Students: Concepts, Measurement, and Causes*, by Jack Citrin and David J. Elkins. ($2.00)
24. *Urban Inequality and Housing Policy in Tanzania: The Problem of Squatting*, by Richard E. Stren. ($2.50)
*25. *The Obsolescence of Regional Integration Theory*, by Ernst B. Haas. ($2.95)
26. *The Voluntary Service Agency in Israel*, by Ralph M. Kramer. ($2.00)
27. *The SOCSIM Demographic-Sociological Microsimulation Program: Operating Manual*, by Eugene A. Hammel et al. ($4.50)
28. *Authoritarian Politics in Communist Europe: Uniformity & Diversity in One-Party States*, edited by Andrew C. Janos. ($3.75)

*International Integration Series

INSTITUTE OF INTERNATIONAL STUDIES MONOGRAPHS (continued)

29. *The Anglo-Icelandic Cod War of 1972-1973: A Case Study of a Fishery Dispute*, by Jeffrey A. Hart. ($2.00)
30. *Plural Societies and New States: A Conceptual Analysis*, by Robert Jackson. ($2.00)
31. *The Politics of Crude Oil Pricing in the Middle East, 1970-1975: A Study in International Bargaining*, by Richard Chadbourn Weisberg. ($3.95)
32. *Agricultural Policy and Performance in Zambia: History, Prospects, and Proposals for Change*, by Doris Jansen Dodge. ($4.95)
33. *Five Classy Programs: Computer Procedures for the Classification of Households*, by E.A. Hammel and R.Z. Deuel. ($3.75)
34. *Housing the Urban Poor in Africa: Policy, Politics, and Bureaucracy in Mombasa*, by Richard E. Stren. ($5.95)
35. *The Russian New Right: Right-Wing Ideologies in the Contemporary USSR*, by Alexander Yanov. ($4.50)
36. *Social Change in Romania, 1860-1940: A Debate on Development in a European Nation*, ed. by Kenneth Jowitt. ($4.50)
37. *The Leninist Response to National Dependency*, by Kenneth Jowitt. ($2.50)
38. *Socialism in Sub-Saharan Africa: A New Assessment*, ed. by Carl G. Rosberg and Thomas M. Callaghy. ($8.50)
39. *Tanzania's Ujamaa Villages: The Implementation of a Rural Development Strategy*, by Dean E. McHenry, Jr. ($5.95)

POLITICS OF MODERNIZATION SERIES

1. *Spanish Bureaucratic-Patrimonialism in America*, by Magali Sarfatti. ($2.00)
2. *Civil-Military Relations in Argentina, Chile, and Peru*, by Liisa North. ($2.00)
3. *Notes on the Process of Industrialization in Argentina, Chile, and Peru*, by Alcira Leiserson. ($1.75)
4. *Chilean Christian Democracy: Politics and Social Forces*, by James Petras. ($1.50)
5. *Social Stratification in Peru*, by Magali S. Larson and Arlene E. Bergman. ($4.95)
6. *Modernization and Coercion*, by Mario Barrera. ($1.50)
7. *Latin America: The Hegemonic Crisis and the Military Coup*, by José Nun. ($2.00)
8. *Development Processes in Chilean Local Government*, by Peter S. Cleaves. ($1.50)
9. *Modernization and Bureaucratic-Authoritarianism: Studies in South American Politics*, by Guillermo A. O'Donnell.

POLICY PAPERS IN INTERNATIONAL AFFAIRS

1. *Images of Detente and the Soviet Political Order*, by Kenneth Jowitt. ($1.00)
2. *Detente After Brezhnev: The Domestic Roots of Soviet Foreign Policy*, by Alexander Yanov. ($3.00)
3. *The Mature Neighbor Policy: A New United States Economic Policy for Latin America*, by Albert Fishlow. ($2.00)
4. *Five Images of the Soviet Future: A Critical Review and Synthesis*, by George W. Breslauer. ($2.50)
5. *Global Evangelism Rides Again: How to Protect Human Rights Without Really Trying*, by Ernst B. Haas. ($2.00)
6. *Israel and Jordan: The Implications of an Adversarial Partnership*, by Ian Lustick. ($2.00)
7. *Political Syncretism in Italy: Historical Coalition Strategies and the Present Crisis*, by Giuseppe Di Palma. ($2.00)
8. *U.S. Foreign Policy in Sub-Saharan Africa: National Interest and Global Strategy*, by Robert M. Price. ($2.25)
9. *East-West Technology Transfer in Perspective*, by R.J. Carrick. ($2.75)

Address correspondence to:
Institute of International Studies
215 Moses Hall
University of California
Berkeley, California 94720